*fire in the sea*

*fire*

# in the sea

## AN ANTHOLOGY OF POETRY AND ART

*Selected by Sue Cowing*

A Kolowalu Book
**UNIVERSITY OF HAWAI'I PRESS**
*in association with*
**The Honolulu Academy of Arts**
**Honolulu**

Library of Congress Cataloging-in-Publication Data
Fire in the sea : an anthology of poetry and art / selected by Sue Cowing.
    p.   cm.
   "A Kolowalu book."
   ISBN 0–8248–1649–8
   1. Poetry—Collections. 2. Pacific Islanders—Poetry. 3. Islands of the Pacific—
Poetry. 4. Oceania—Poetry. 5. Children's poetry. I. Cowing, Sue, 1938– .
  PN6110.P2F57   1996
  808.81—dc20                      95–42546

01 00 99 98 97 96  5 4 3 2 1

All works of art in this book were photographed by Tibor Franyo, with the exception
of the Hawaiian koa bowl on pg. 14, photographed by Hugo DeVries

*Front cover:* Pin by Elizabeth Garrison, *Volcano Dream No. 4.*
*Title page:* Mixed media print by Louis Pohl, *Crater #3.*
*Back cover:* Detail of a blown glass pilgrim flask, Roman Empire.

Designed by Brian Ellis Martin with assistance from Susan E. Kelly
Produced by Marquand Books, Inc., Seattle
Printed in Singapore

# contents

13  *fire in the wood*

29  *i couldn't think straight, so thought crooked*

## 45  my father remembered what it was to be small

## 57  owls started this

## i may be silent, but...

## the minute i heard my first love story

## 99   what is the opposite of riot?

## 109   i thought the earth remembered me

## 129    *the afternoon swam by*

# preface

Just as flowing lava turns the ocean to steam and keeps on burning—fire in the sea—the best poems we hear or read take surprising, even "impossible," turns that change the way we see the world afterward. Poets and visual artists try to say what we would have thought could not be expressed, and when they succeed, we share their deep pleasure. If this book allows its readers to regain that pleasure or to feel it perhaps for the first time, it will have achieved its purpose.

I have taken particular care to choose poems that will be meaningful to young readers. Since most people over the age of ten can enjoy a wide range of poetry, I have selected few poems written expressly for the young. Most of the poems presented here were written in English; the rest have been translated into English from their original Asian, Pacific, and European languages. The illustrations are from the permanent collections of the Honolulu Academy of Arts and include a few pieces by young students of art at the academy, retained over the years for the lending collection at Linekona. It is my hope that pairing poems with art will make the experience of each doubly memorable. I chose the poems first, then the art to illustrate them, looking for connections in feeling and imagination rather than merely literal illustration.

This anthology includes, I believe for the first time, a significant sample of Pacific poetry in an international collection. The Pacfic islands have long poetic traditions, and the last two decades have seen a lively outpouring of contemporary poetry, especially in Fiji, Hawai`i, New Zealand, and Samoa, that deserves to be better known within and beyond the region.* Meanwhile, as Nicholas Hasluck says in his poem: "Islands which have/never existed/have made their way/onto maps nevertheless."

Carl Sandburg once described poetry as "the journal of a sea animal living on land, wanting to fly in the air." Such animals live everywhere—on islands, on coasts, and, like Sandburg, in the middle of continents. Some of their flights may be found in this book.

*For this reason, I have indicated "Hawai`i" rather than simply "USA" under the names of the poets and artists from this island state, even though the other poets and artists are identified by country.

# acknowledgments

I would like to extend thanks to a few of
the many people who offered their assis-
tance and encouragement during the years
this book was in the making: Iris Wiley,
Sharon Yamamoto, and Cheri Dunn of the
University of Hawai'i Press; George Ellis,
Jennifer Saville, Sanna Deutsch, Tibor
Franyo, and Pauline Sugino of the Hono-
lulu Academy of Arts; Cedric Cowing;
Nancy Kwok; Tony Quagliano; Joseph
Stanton; Vilsoni Hereniko; Norma Gorst;
and the students of La Pietra Hawai'i
School for Girls, especially Janet Austin.

# fire in the wood

**p**oetry is the best language we have for talking about mystery. People have always turned to poetry to celebrate and account for the origins of things or to acknowledge unseen powers at work in the world.

## Fire in the Wood

The wood has fire in it.
It has just come back to life.
Can you argue that wood has no fire in it
When rubbing brings out these flames?

NGO CHAN LUU (19TH CENTURY)
Vietnam
Translated by Burton Raffel

Ron Kent, Hawai'i
*Bowl*, 1988
Norfolk Island pine

Koa bowl, Hawai'i
19th century

## Taaroa

He was there—Taaroa was his name.
Around him void:
no earth no sky
no sea no people.
Taaroa calls—there is no echo.
In his loneliness he changes himself into the world.
These entangled roots are Taaroa.
These rocks are Taaroa.
Taaroa: sand of the sea.
Taaroa: clarity.
Taaroa: seed.
Taaroa: ground.
Taaroa the eternal
the powerful
creator of the world
the large sacred world
the world
which is only the shell.
Taaroa is the life inside it.

TAHITIAN TRADITIONAL POEM
English version by Ulli Beier

## Island

from *Short Songs*

This island was a frail tremor snared
in stingray seas dark with threat of storm.
The tremor was strong enough
to give us birth.

ALBERT WENDT (1939–)
Samoa

Elizabeth Garrison, USA
*Volcano Dream No. 4,* 1985
Pin: sterling silver, copper,
glass, enamel, old bone,
and cloisonné

15

## Birth of Sea and Land Life

from *The Kumulipo**

The night gave birth

Born was Kumulipo in the night, a male

Born was Poʻele in the night, a female

Born was the coral polyp, born was the coral, came forth

Born was the grub that digs and heaps up the earth, came forth

Born was his [child] an earthworm, came forth

Born was the starfish, his child the small starfish came forth

Born was the sea cucumber, his child the small sea cucumber came forth

Born was the sea urchin, the sea urchin [tribe]

Born was the short-spiked sea urchin, came forth

Born was the smooth sea urchin, his child the long-spiked came forth

Born was the ring-shaped sea urchin, his child the thin-spiked came forth

Born was the barnacle, his child the pearl oyster came forth

Born was the mother-of-pearl, his child the oyster came forth

Born was the mussel, his child the hermit crab came forth

Born was the big limpet, his child the small limpet came forth

Born was the cowry, his child the small cowry came forth

Born was the naka shellfish, the rock oyster his child came forth

Born was the drupa shellfish, his child the bitter white shellfish came forth

Born was the conch shell, his child the small conch shell came forth

Born was the nerita shellfish, the sand-burrowing shellfish his child
    came forth

Born was the fresh water shellfish, his child the small fresh water shellfish
    came forth

Born was man for the narrow stream, the woman for the broad stream

Born was the Ekaha moss living in the sea

Guarded by the Ekahakaha fern living on land

Darkness slips into light

Earth and water are the food of the plant

The god enters, man cannot enter

Man for the narrow stream, woman for the broad stream

TRADITIONAL HAWAIIAN GENEALOGICAL PRAYER CHANT (CA. 1700)
Translated by Martha Warren Beckwith

*The Kumulipo* is a chant of over two thousand lines. This selection is
from the earliest section dealing with "Po," or night.

## Moana

Name of the Great Ocean
the dark blue sea
the mysterious
Moana-Nui-o-Kiva*
Moana-Vai-a-Vare†
mysterious ocean
Moana our daughter
graceful rider through space
from Havaiki
today you have earned
the keys to enter
the four rooms
of the mysterious
ocean of life
many will call upon
your name for guidance
for interpretation
of these mysteries
Moana our sister
you were born and raised
in the mysterious ocean

Madge Tennent, Hawai'i
*Three Head and Shoulders Studies,* 1954
Blue water-soluble pencil and wash

we look to you for understanding
of the fish we eat
the waves that destroy us
the waves that create new lands
for us
Moana our daughter
Moana our sister
Moana our mother

KAURAKA KAURAKA (1951–)
Cook Islands

*The Pacific Ocean.
†Means "myth" or "mysterious ocean."

18

## Turtle and Coconut

One stormy night a pregnant turtle
crawled ashore to lay her eggs
under a coconut tree
As the turtle's nose
touched the coconut roots
the tree said, "Stop your tickling.
I'm trying to sleep!"
"Forgive me Coconut; can I lay my eggs
among your roots? It's no longer safe
out in the open sand."
Coconut knew
some of his roots would be severed
to make a hole for the eggs.
"You can dig your hole Turtle,
but promise me that only I
can eat the egg-shells of your young.
Agreed?"
"Agreed."
Four thousand eggs were laid between
   the roots
and the coconut tree cared for them
as if they were his own.

     KAURAKA KAURAKA (1951–)
     Cook Islands

Ansel Adams, USA
*Roots, Foster Garden,* 1948
Vintage silver gelatin print

The roots in this photograph
are banyan.

19

Gwendolyn Morris at age 12, Hawai'i
Untitled print, 1955

## The River Flows Back

In my mother's womb
peace was mine
but I said *"maping."*＊
I greeted the light
and came into the world,
saluting it with a cry.
I paddled downstream
drifting at ease
like Adam before the fall.

But now
a storm rises before me
my canoe has swung around
I paddle against the stream.
The river my helper
has become my enemy

I fight the river
until my veins stand out
until the paddle blisters my palms.

Yet in this battle I gain glory
I win fame
I grow a name
the true essence of it.
One day I will reach the source again
There at my beginnings
another peace
 will welcome me.

KUMALAU TAWALI
Papua New Guinea

＊Term of greeting in the Manus language.

# Long Ago . . .

Long ago, on a journey
I discovered a river:
it was scarcely a child, a dog, a bird,
that newly born river.
It was gurgling and moaning
among the stones
of the iron-stained sierra:
it was begging for life
between the solitudes of sky and snow,
in the distance, high up.
I was as weary
as an old horse
next to the wild creature
that was beginning to run,
to jump and to grow,
to sing with a clear voice,
to know the earth,
stones, passing time,
to travel night and day,
to become thunder,
until getting dizzy,
until entering the calm,
until growing wide and bringing water,
until becoming patriarchal and sailed upon,
this small river,
small and clumsy as a metallic fish
shedding its scales as it passes,
drops of assaulted silver,
a river
crying to be born,

growing before my eyes.
There in the mountain ranges of my country
at times and long ago
I saw, touched and heard
that which was being born:
a heartbeat, a sound among the stones
was that which was being born.

PABLO NERUDA (1904–1973)
Chile
Translated by William O'Daly

Jules Tavernier, France
*Wailuku Falls, Hilo*, 1886
Pastel

Water
needs no feet
heals itself

PHILIPPINE SAYING

Aztec rattle in the form of a
standing woman, 900–1200
Clay

## Ultimate Problems

In the Aztec design God crowds
into the little pea that is rolling
out of the picture.
All the rest extends bleaker
because God has gone away.

In the White Man design, though,
no pea is there.
God is everywhere,
but hard to see.
The Aztecs frown at this.

*How do you know he is everywhere?*
*And how did he get out of the pea?*

WILLIAM STAFFORD (1914–1993)
USA

## Kitchen Philosophy

"What is God?" I was four feet tall
When mother stopped, a pewter mug
Frozen on her apron, the wall
Behind us wondrous with crockery.
Had I pulled the wrong plug?
Later she smiled, smiling gave me
An onion. "Inside is what
You're looking for." I thought she joked,
But peeled until my eyes ran wet.
For days afterward I moped,
Cursed mothers and their endless fibs;
Now see the purpose of mortal ribs.

SUDESH MISHRA (1962–)
Fiji

## Looking thru Those Eye-holes

once an artist went overseas
his father died in his absence
& was buried in the village

he followed a rainbow upon his return
& came to a cemetery
he dug in search of reality
till he broke his father's skull
to wear its fore-half as a mask

try it/look through those eye-holes
see the old paintings/view the world
in the way the dead had done

RUSSELL SOABA (1950–)
Papua New Guinea

23

# The Great Bird of Love over the Kingdom

I want to become a great night bird
Called The Zimmer, grow intricate gears
And tendons, brace my wings on updrafts,
Roll them down with a motion
That lifts me slowly to the stars
To fly above the troubles of the kingdom.
When I soar the moon will shine past
My shoulder and slide through
Streams like a luminous fish.
I want my cry to be huge and melancholy,
The undefiled movement of my wings
To fold and unfold in the rising gloom.

People will see my silhouette from
Their  windows and be comforted,
Knowing that, though oppressed,
They are cherished and watched over,
Can turn to kiss their children,
Tuck them into their beds and say:
    Sleep tight.
    No harm tonight,
    In starry skies
    The Zimmer flies.

PAUL ZIMMER (1934–)
USA

Anonymous artist, Papua
New Guinea
Stopper for a lime container,
mid-20th century
Wood and traces of
paint, sennit, and shell

25

# i thank You God for most this amazing

Litany

He is the green of the rice paddy fields,
He's the gold of ripening corn,
He is the blue of the iridescent sea,
He's the flame that rekindles the dawn.
He is the roar of the roller-taming reef,
And the sigh of the sea-lipping breeze,
He is the caw of the *koki** taking fright,
And the coo of a dove in the trees.
He is the scent on a frangipani bloom,
He's the sweetness of lush sugarcane.
He is the softness of the kapok's downy floss,
He's the freshness of afternoon rain.
He is the essence of all He has wrought.
He needs none to further His plan.
Ban, vain mortals, the blasphemous thought
That God needs the worship of man.

RAYMOND PILLAI (1942–)
Fiji

*Parrot.

i thank You God for most this amazing
day:for the leaping greenly spirits of trees
and a blue dream of sky;and for everything
which is natural which is infinite which is yes

(i who have died am alive again today,
and this is the sun's birthday;this is the birth
day of life and love and wings;and of the gay
great happening illimitably earth)

how should tasting touching hearing seeing
breathing any—lifted from the no
of all nothing—human merely being
doubt unimaginable You?

(now the ears of my ears awake and
now the eyes of my eyes are opened)

E. E. CUMMINGS (1894–1962)
USA

Janet Coons at age 16, Hawai`i
Untitled collage

## Walking Westward in the Morning

walking westward in the morning the sun follows from behind
I walk following my lengthened shadow before me
the sun and I don't argue about which one of us creates the shadow
the shadow and I don't argue about which one of us must lead the way

SAPARDI DJOKO DAMONO (1940–)
Indonesia
Translated by John H. McGlynn

27

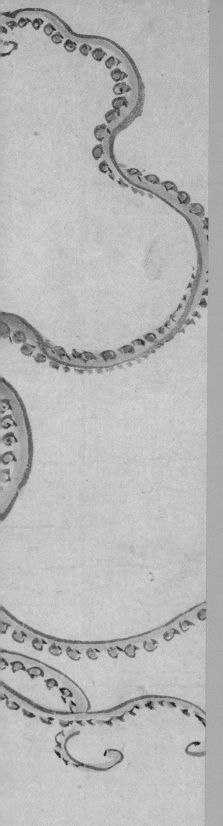

# i couldn't think straight, so thought crooked

Our creative imagination is not limited by the "facts" of daily life, but can see ordinary things in fresh and startling ways. Often this means being able to picture a different reality, to accept two opposite truths at once, or to combine the waking world with the world of dreams.

## Water Monster

Sure I saw the water monster!
Why do you think I got back here so fast?
Yes, that was me
sitting in a tree by the lake
wishing myself into a walking stick
and making cracking-leaves sounds
and making wishes on myself.
That's when I saw him!
I couldn't think straight so thought crooked,
which is how I got to be
a snake
come winding out
and safe at home.
All because I saw him.

> HOWARD NORMAN (1949–)
> USA

Kawanabe Kyosai (Gyosai), Japan
*Vignettes on the Theme Demons and Gods*
(detail), late 1870s
Ink and color on paper

Ann McCoy, USA
*Iguanas*, 1979
Lithograph and colored pencil

## Mo'o

My son isn't afraid of lizards.
He catches the fat mo'o in our house,
caresses the fear out of them,
and releases them into the garden.

I've never told him our ancestors
believed lizards were gods.

ALBERT WENDT (1939–)
Samoa

## Mo'okini Heiau

*—for Kalani*

Many died at Mo'okini,*
four hundred and four hundred and four hundred and on.
I walked through the abandoned fields
and looked for you.
I wore the helmet of forty thousand mo'o,
four hundred and four hundred and on;
the sun was setting. I sat on the high walls
on the stone heaped for centuries.
I added the sunsets since the last death.
Where is power?
The sun falls into the sea,
the sea beats the stones
and the stones turn to crickets who
carry me away on the beat of their song,
and I am talking to you tonight.

We keep singing. The stones break beneath us.

MARTHA WEBB (1946–)
Hawai'i

*Mo'okini Heiau is a large ancient Hawaiian temple on the island of Hawai'i. It is said to have been built by passing large waterworn stones hand over hand from Pololu Valley.

32

## Bread of Dreams

Last night
I dared to eat the bread of dreams.
I don't know how the sky
Came to hear about it.

Big wings heard the news
Long beaks heard the news
Cruel teeth heard the news
Sharp claws heard the news.

The bread was quite naked
Its flavor was quite naked
It had no covering of soul
And no covering of flesh.

One swoop and the bread is snatched away
My hands are torn
One swoop and my cheeks are scarred.

On my lips no bread
Only talk of bread.
Nights are black vultures.

Last night
I dared to eat the bread of dreams.
I don't know how the sky
came to hear about it.

AMRITA PRITAM (1919–)
India

Joseph Feher, Hawai'i
*Night of the 'Iwa*, 1978
Etching

33

Louis Pohl, Hawai'i
*Crater #3,* 1972
Mixed media print

## Ghislaine's Quilt

The first sketches came when I was away.
I don't know if it started
more from her dream
or the real volcano she owns
a piece of, which recently
overflowed to the sea.
But the quilt I look down
every night in bed,
is a patchwork mountain
of blacks and greys like different
days of cooling lava,
abstract shapes like burnt

leaves scattering, and gobs of red
paisley oozing fat tears
from the open mouth
which seems to be
waiting for stars to fall
from the background of
symmetrical sky.
Sometimes I'm at the peak,
underneath the sky in my sleep.
Sometimes I'm receiving the red flow
into my mouth, which, she says,
always opens when I dream.

ERIC CHOCK (1950–)
Hawai'i

## The Door on Its Hinges

*—Volcano, Hawai'i*

The arc of earth
rises burning: the weight of its fall
shows it to be stone, though alight,
and the grass is bleached
bright after prayer.

Now the path across the brown and black stones:
sit down to wait, and the stones begin
to tilt and crawl.

The path, torn across
by a ridge of recent fire,
rises and goes again over the new hills,

hills a line of spread hood
left by the rock sinking back, still alive,

and there is another path
which follows the fire down. At its edge,
half under the hood, look up, there are a hundred thousand
cross-legged figures fired orange and red
which are only rock once molten.

Return then to the pit: stand at its edge
looking down to the weight of new boulders
far below and see it rise
and think yourself falling, and step back
with the hook of the light in you

with the door, swinging wide on its hinges,
a light.

MARTHA WEBB (1946–)
Hawai'i

## A Hot Day

on a hot day i think
everything is an accident
and things being what they aren't
i have sometimes stood along
corridors and seen the world
spinning on its axis

and the child's distant balloon
is a little globe
attached to a string
with a bigger blue balloon
of the sky stretched behind

ARTHUR YAP
Singapore

35

Shōtei Hokuju, Japan
*Monkey Bridge*, early 1820s
Woodblock print

## Sleep Is like a Bridge

Sleep is like a bridge
which reaches from today to tomorrow.
Below, like a dream,
the water flows by.

JUAN RAMÓN JIMÉNEZ (1881–1958)
Spain

## Don't Go Back to Sleep

The breezes at dawn have secrets to tell you.
　　Don't go back to sleep!
You must ask for what you really want.
　　Don't go back to sleep!
　People are going back and forth
Across the doorsill where the two worlds touch,
　　The door is round and open.
　　Don't go back to sleep.

RUMI (1207–1273)
Persia
Translated by Coleman Barks and John Maynor

Fish shop—
how cold the lips
of the salted bream.

MATSUO BASHŌ
(1644–1694)
Japan

## The Brook

First time I passed the brook it filled my eye.
The second time it was a tiny snake.
The next few times I only heard it cry
Behind me and I was afraid for my own sake.

G. BURCE BUNAO (1926–)
Philippines

36

## The Fish in the Attic

They refuse to come down.
They refuse to say
what they are doing up there.

You go up the ladder to coax them,
you get their silent, openmouthed
stare through the trapdoor.
The secret they've always kept
they're keeping higher,
near the roof of the house.

They investigate old trunks,
their flat noses bumping the locks,
looking for letters
still wet with emotion
after all these years.

They pretend they can live there
forever, swimming, flying
to the peak of the attic
in a gesture of getting water.

At night, as you sleep,
they pass over your head,
making an untranslatable
pattern amidst
what you have discarded
or do not know you need yet.

On a cold morning,
when ice has formed on the roof,
you will find them
huddled near the beams,
strangely waiting
for a fisherman to cut the hole
they can escape through.

PHILIP DACEY (1939–)
USA

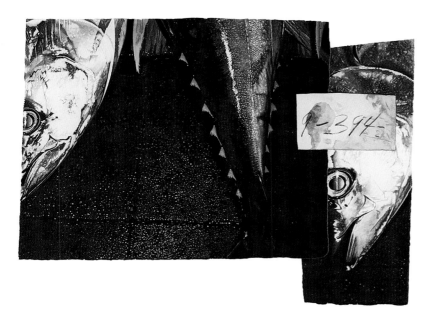

Doug Young, Hawai'i
*Ahi*, 1977
Watercolor

## A Game

They are throwing the ball
to and fro between them,
in and out of the picture.
She is in the painting
hung on the wall
in a narrow gold frame.
He stands on the floor
catching and tossing
at the right distance.
She wears a white dress,
black boots and stockings,
and a flowered straw hat.
She moves in silence
but it seems from her face
that she must be laughing.
Behind her is sunlight
and a tree-filled garden;
you might think to hear
birds or running water,
but no, there is nothing.
Once or twice he has spoken
but does so no more,
for she cannot answer.

Henri Toulouse-Lautrec,
France
*May Milton*, 1895
Color lithograph

So he stands smiling,
playing her game
(she is almost a child),
not daring to go,
intent on the ball.
And she is the same.
For what would result
neither wishes to know
if it should fall.

FLEUR ADCOCK (1934–)
New Zealand

38

## Stone

Go inside a stone.
That would be my way.
Let somebody else become a dove
Or gnash with a tiger's tooth.
I am happy to be a stone.

From the outside a stone is a riddle:
No one knows how to answer it.
Yet within, it must be cool and quiet
Even though a cow steps on it full weight,
Even though a child throws it in a river;
The stone sinks, slow, unperturbed
To the river bottom
Where the fishes come to knock on it
And listen.

I have seen sparks fly out
When two stones are rubbed,
So perhaps it is not dark inside after all;
Perhaps there is a moon shining
From somewhere, as though behind a hill —
Just enough light to make out
The strange writings, the star-charts
On the inner walls.

CHARLES SIMIC (1938–)
USA

Churinga cult stone,
Aranda tribe, Central
Australia, pre-European
Gray slate and red pigment

# Islands

Islands which have
never existed
have made their way
onto maps nevertheless.

And having done so
have held their place,
quite respectably,
sometimes for centuries.

Voyages of undiscovery, deep
into the charted wastes,
were then required
to move them off.

The Auroras, for instance.
Beneath Cape Horn.
Sighted first in 1762
and confirmed by

Reuben Tam, Hawai'i
*Islanding: Limestone,* 1989
From *Archipelago Series* #6
Acrylic on paper

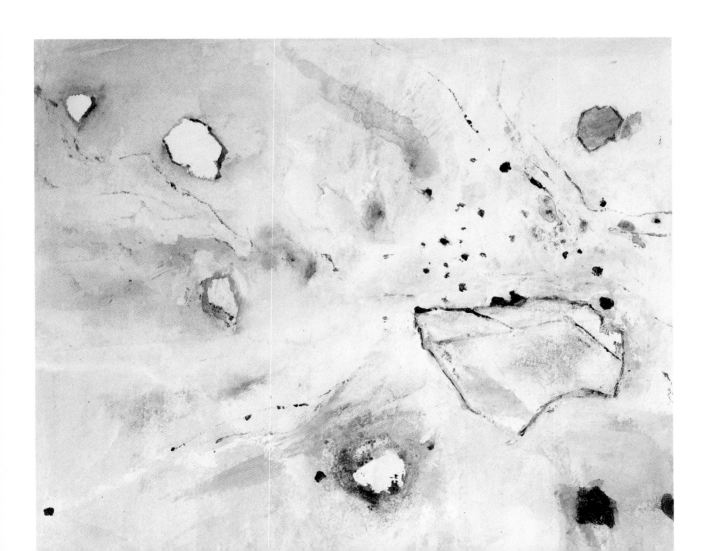

Captain Manuel de Oyarvido
thirty years later.

But since the voyage of
someone whose name
escapes me, on a date
I can't quite remember—
they are now known
not to exist.

Cartographers—hands high
in the frail rigging of
latitudes and longitudes—
wiped them out, reluctantly.

And so, some mariners
who pushed beyond the pale,
forfeit the names they left
in lonely seas.

Remember them
Respect their enterprise.
It takes a certain
kind of boldness
to have seen such
islands first of all.

In the mind's atlas,
footnotes, like broken rules,
are not without importance.

Who found America?

Those canny trawlers,
absent for months,
fishing the depths,
must have been somewhere
with their sealed lips.

NICHOLAS HASLUCK (1942–)
Australia

## School Policy on Stickmen

It's said that children should not use
stick figures when they draw!
And yet I've lain all night awake
looking at this drawing here
of orange men, stick figures every one of them,
walking up a crayon mountain hand in hand
walking up my wall.

They're edging up a ridge
their backs against a mountain
pinned against my wall.
And every one is smiling.
They know the way a mountain laughs,
especially crayon mountains made of brown.
They know they're not allowed,
these orange men.

SAM HUNT (1946–)
New Zealand

41

# When

Once upon a time when there was no time,
when no one had any need for time because there was plenty of it,
when time was an idea whose time hadn't come,
when the pear tree produced peaches or toy trucks,
when fleas jumped into the sky wearing very heavy shoes,
when everybody ate what they cooked and scientists were always sick
because they had to eat bombs,
when dogs and cats were on the best of terms
and men and women never fought pitched battles
under the pitched tent,
when children never took baths because they were always swimming,
there lived a very old storyteller
in a village high in the mountains
who told a very long story
day and night.
No one knew when he had begun telling this story
because he was always telling it
and you could drop by his house and listen to some of it
and then come back when you were old yourself
and listen to some more of it.
When I heard him the story hadn't even begun because he was
still busy telling when the story began.
Maybe, one day, we should drop in on him and listen some more,
maybe he has begun.
We will, okay, one day, when we have the time.

ANDREI CODRESCU (1946–)
USA

42

Shibata Zeshin, Japan
*Jurojin, Deer, and Tortoise in Landscape,*
scroll, 1889
Color on silk

Shibata Zeshin was not only a
painter but also a printmaker, an
acclaimed master of lacquer, and
a haiku poet.

The door marked Good
sticks

CHINESE SAYING

# my father remembered what it was to be small

**f**amilies are unforgettable. Many of
the most expressive poems and works of
art draw on the deep feelings between
fathers, mothers, and children: love, fear,
admiration, tenderness.

Knife can't whittle
its own handle.

KOREAN SAYING

## In the Giant's Castle

My father remembered what it was to be small,
And to nourish rebellion.
My father in the night concocted
From vinegar, brown paper, pepper,
A hot plaster for my jumping ear,
Which was much the same as waving a wand.
I could show you my tommy-axed finger
Bound together without stitches,

Or tell you how my father became a wall
And relied on me to stand as firm
While a doctor scissored off my crushed nail.
But when I grew, and climbed
The hill Difficulty, and at length
Came face to face with Giant Despair,
My father was not there.
Just his initials marked on a stone.

RUTH DALLAS (1919–)
New Zealand

Suit of samurai armor
Japan, 1346
Iron, leather, lacquer, silk,
brocade, and gilding

## Poem for My Father

I lie dreaming
when my father comes to me and says,
I hope you write a book someday.
He thinks I waste my time,
but outside, he spends hours over stones,
gauging the size and shape a rock will take
to fill a space,
to make a wall of dreams around our home.
In the house he built with his own hands
I wish for the lure that catches all fish
or girls with hair like long moss in the river.
His thoughts are just as far and old
as the lava chips like flint off the hammer,
and he sees the mold of dreams
taking shape in his hands.
His eyes see across orchids on the wall,
into black rock, down to the sea,
and he remembers the harbor full of fish,
orchids in the hair of women thirty years before
he thought of me, this home, or stone walls.
Some rocks fit perfectly, slipping into place
with light taps of his hammer.
He thinks of me inside
and takes a big slice of stone,
pounds it into the ground
to make the corner of the wall.
I cannot wake until I bring
the fish and the girl home.

ERIC CHOCK (1950–)
Hawai`i

Joseph Feher, Hawai`i
Etching from *Voices on the Wind*, 1955

## Human Affection

Mother, I love you so.
Said the child, I love you more than I know.
She laid her head on her mother's arm,
And the love between them kept them warm.

STEVIE SMITH (1902–1971)
England

Mary Cassatt, USA
*The Child's Caress*, 1891
Oil on canvas

## Next Time

Gingko trees live 1,000 years.
Eating the leaves will clear your brain.
When I heard about them, I thought of my mother,
how much I would like to sit under one with her
in the ancient shade, nibbling
the flesh, the stem, the central vein.

NAOMI SHIHAB NYE (1952–)
USA

# ʻAwapuhi

Mama loved the scent
of the wild yellow ginger,
growing thick on the slopes of Tantalus.

In its blooming season,
she would walk up that steep, curvey road
to pick two or three.

These she would weave into a brooch,
to be pinned to the inside
of her blouse—hidden,
but for that warm perfume.

On the day she was buried
she wore a lei of wild yellow ginger,
freshly picked from the slopes of Tantalus,

And left for me,
in a blue shoe box,
a thousand, neatly woven, dry,
        fragrant brooches.

> PUANANI BURGESS (1947–)
> Hawaiʻi

John Young, Hawaiʻi
*The Red Béret*, 1945
Oil on canvas

49

## Another Life

A seal swam toward me
in a dream
I saw it under the ice
following me
with my mother's face
so that's where she
went when she left us
we thought she would have
gone to a warmer place
an ocean the color of new leaves
instead I saw her
circling beneath the house
and the water in the cooking pots
boiled twice that night

DANA NAONE HALL (1949–)
Hawai'i

## Teu

Mother, you were there
        at the passage
                when our ship arrived.
The sea, heavy as oil,
        heaved unbroken
                on the reef,
the stars
        lay in clusters
                on the water,
and you wept
        when you laid
                the Southern Cross
upon our eyes.

ALISTAIR CAMPBELL (1922–)
New Zealand

Anonymous Inuit artist
Eskimo seal sculpture, ca. 1970
Steatite

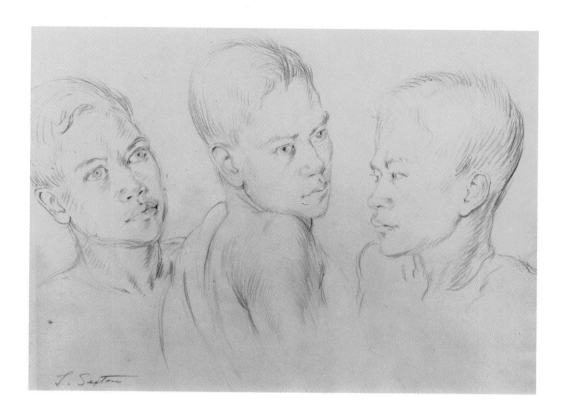

Lloyd Sexton, USA
*Three Heads*, 1952
Pencil drawing

## My Mother's Humming

I grew my hair long because my son
needed a mother and I remembered
fondly my mother's long white hair.
I stayed at home because no one else
would be there with him. We played.
I remembered too that my mother's play
was to be within humming distance as she
let me play alone. She was small and slight
—I knew that—but to my son I am huge
and indestructible; he learns to tackle me.

I was always clothed; he is mostly naked.
I was pale; he is the color of wet earth.
His mother calls sometimes long distance. I
hum as my Mom did so he'll know where I am.

JOHN ENRIGHT (1945–)
Samoa

51

## Son

My son as a tree
as a shadow of the tree
in the moonlight as
the trade wind that
shivers that shadow that
ring's Kali's chimes at
the corner of the porch
as he rolls over with a
sigh against the night &
a dream-purple cry
its cause and its squall
all forgotten at dawn when
that tree is but one tree
among many and he is awake,
      my son.

  JOHN ENRIGHT (1945–)
  Samoa

## Who's Who

That child—
  Of another's house—
Eats a lot,
Dances like a monkey.

This child—
  Of my house—
Eats lotus buds,
Dances like a lord.

   FROM THE BENGALI ORAL TRADITION

Shibata Zeshin, Japan
*Monkey Posing as a
Collector*, ca. 1835
Ink and color on silk

Pierre Mignard, France
*Portrait of Three Children*, 1647
Oil on canvas

## Clouds on the Sea

I walk among men with tall bones,
With shoes of leather, and pink faces;
I meet no man holding a begging bowl;
All have their dwelling places.

In my country
Every child is taught to read and write,
Every child has shoes and a warm coat,
Every child must eat his dinner,
No one must grow any thinner;
It is considered remarkable and not nice
To meet bed-bugs or lice.
Oh we live like the rich
With music at the touch of a switch,
Light in the middle of the night,
Water in the house as if from a spring.

Hot, if you wish, or cold, anything
For the comfort of the flesh,
In my country. Fragment
Of new skin at the edge of the world's ulcer.

For the question
That troubled you as you watched the reapers
And a poor woman following,
Gleaning the ears on the ground,
*Why should I have grain and this woman none?*
No satisfactory answer has been found.

RUTH DALLAS (1919–)
New Zealand

The ears are brothers
but never see each other

PHILIPPINE SAYING

## Before We Go

We are walking, my sister
ahead by three years, and me

zooming slowly
(slightly above ground but
still apparently touching it)
down the rutted puddle track

until the secret place she knows
where no dream is abandoned

by decay: rotting buses!
fiery trucks with burnisht trays!

we climb in through the window
of a cadillac, remembering to turn

the ignition, engage reverse and
check for redback spiders before we go.

RICHARD TIPPING (1949–)
Australia

## For My Brother

You were born
in the year of the fish,
during the rainy month
when the pond brims over
and the trees in the gulch
grow leaves like spinach
and mold thickens
under the skin.

I was two
when from the broken water,
you came swimming,
slippery and smooth,
barely bigger than a tadpole.
You jumped
into father's surprised hands.
Mother wrestled to keep
your jellied body
cradled in her arm.

What a thirsty baby,
wanting seawater instead of milk,
you flipped happily in the crib
after your mushroom mouth
went slack, satisfied.

Peering into the cage of your crib,
I clung to the bars
while you slept,
the soft bones of your head
pared streamline in shape

Tadatoshi, Japan
*Mermaid*, late 18th century
Netsuke, ivory

as though in your dream
you swam through the air.

I watched your eyes gradually
slope back toward your ears,
your cheeks curved like slender islands.
How I envied that profile:
Egyptian and remote
like a delicate water-bearer of the Nile.

I carried you
through the mud to the stream
where crayfish were lobsters,
palm fronds umbrellas,
and watched you maneuver
in the stream,
pouring silver tongue to surface,
then diving once again
to navigate without words.

We each have become our own animals.
I am like the sheep,
woolly and silent.
I plant my belly on the hillside,
count myself to sleep.
I sit in the sun,
patient as a boulder,
like any proper sister.
And I know that I move differently,
using the alphabet
to spring from me an ocean,
to propel me through night waters.
This is my way
of swimming with you.

CATHY SONG (1955–)
Hawai'i

# owls started this

**W**e have always suspected that animals, our fellow creatures, know something that has meaning for our lives, and we often portray ourselves as animals, or animals acting like us.

Munakata Shiko, Japan
*Owl on a Branch*, 1965
Ink and color on paper

## Always Surprised

Owls started this.

When this boy went owl looking
it was night.  He would hear one
up ahead
and squint his eyes to try and see it.

He tried to catch one
by not making noise.

Then that owl called at him
from BEHIND!
And he jumped.

He only heard owls from behind.

Always fooled by owls,
which was, in later days, the cause
of his name.  He got jumpy.
Even if a leaf fell on his shoulder
he jumped, JUMPED as if he was
always being surprised.

Or the first drop
of rain he felt, too,
he'd turn and say
"WHICH OWL SPIT THAT ON ME?"

Even in daylight.

HOWARD NORMAN (1949–)
USA

## Bats

A bat is born
Naked and blind and pale.
His mother makes a pocket of her tail
And catches him. He clings to her long fur
By his thumbs and toes and teeth.
And then the mother dances through
   the night
Doubling and looping, soaring,
   somersaulting—
Her baby hangs on underneath.
All night, in happiness, she hunts and flies.
Her high sharp cries
Like shining needlepoints of sound
Go out into the night and, echoing back,
Tell her what they have touched.
She hears how far it is, how big it is,
Which way it's going:
She lives by hearing.
The mother eats the moths and gnats
   she catches

In full flight; in full flight
The mother drinks the water of the pond
She skims across. Her baby hangs on tight.
Her baby drinks the milk she makes him
In moonlight or starlight, in mid air.
Their single shadow, printed on the moon
Or fluttering across the stars,
Whirls on all night; at daybreak
The tired mother flaps home to her rafter.
The others all are there.
They hang themselves up by their toes.
They wrap themselves in their brown wings.
Bunched upside down, they sleep in air.
Their sharp ears, their sharp teeth, their quick
   sharp faces
Are dull and slow and mild.
All the bright day, as the mother sleeps,
She folds her wings about her sleeping child.

RANDALL JARRELL (1914–1965)
USA

59

## You Can Go Very Far at That

The 1st time I learned to spell elephant I was transported,
    the elephant thanked me,
I rode on him until I could spell India and Hindu and
    "do you love me?"
again the elephant answered yes and this time with a
    chorus of tigers,
soon I was able to spell Blake and forests and the world
    increased in wonder,
I didn't want to stop riding, it was great to be up there
    and I was really dressed up
and there were festivals in every village that I entered.
    When I opened a book birds flew out
    or rabbits came out of a word.
Then I saw a procession of elephants and even the Buddha.

JOHN TAGLIABUE (1923–)
USA

Rajasthan, India
*Ganesha*, 10th century
Pink sandstone

Ganesha, the elephant-headed god of India,
brings good luck, health, and success to all.

## The Shark

My sweet, let me tell you about the shark.
Though his eyes are bright, his thought is dark.
He's quiet—that speaks well of him.
So does the fact that he can swim.
But though he swims without a sound,
Wherever he swims he looks around
With those two bright eyes and that one dark thought.
He has only one, but he thinks it a lot.
And the thought he thinks but can never complete
Is his long dark thought of something to eat.
Most anything does, and I have to add
That when he eats his manners are bad.
He's a gulper, a ripper, a snatcher, a grabber.
Yes, his manners are drab. But his thought is drabber.
That one dark thought he can never complete
Of something—anything—somehow to eat.

Be careful where you swim, my sweet.

JOHN CIARDI (1916–1986)
USA

Ceremonial staff (detail)
Solomon Islands, pre-European
Wood, mother-of-pearl inlay

## Epigram

I fish for minnows in the lake.
Just born, they have no fear of man.
And those who have learned,
Never come back to warn them.

SU TUNG P'O (1036–1101)
China
Translated by Kenneth Rexroth

Telling a fish
about water

BURMESE SAYING

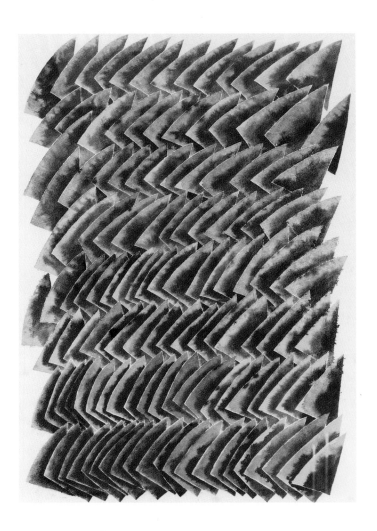

Minoru Ōhira, Japan
*Untitled*, 1953
Graphite and ink wash on paper

Tongue

pale pig

in a bone fence

PHILIPPINE SAYING

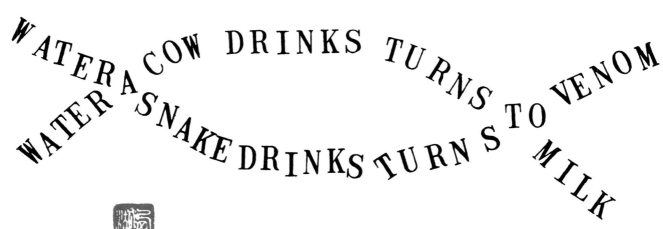

WATER A COW DRINKS TURNS TO VENOM

WATER A SNAKE DRINKS TURNS TO MILK

WAYNE WESTLAKE (1947–1984)
Hawai`i

Smart
a cat rolling an egg.

KOREAN SAYING

Utagawa Hiroshige, Japan
*Asakusa Rice Fields*, 1856–1858
From *One Hundred Views of Edo*
Woodblock print

## To Puffin, a White Cat

On the dark blue rug that is a midnight sky
The creamy saucer fills its heaven like a moon,
And over it a cat's white face
Basks in a muted ecstasy,
Lapping the milky way to paradise
With near-shut golden eyes, pearled beard and rosy mouth,
A cosy mask, lit by contentment from within
And by reflected radiance from beneath;
Where, like true benevolence, eclipsing its material cause,
The saucer, empty, still illuminates,
While Puffin sits and contemplates
Infinity's great O, the starry silk
Of dreams that only can be patched with milk.

Until the want is satisfied, for joy he softly roars,
And kneads his milky firmament with omnipresent paws.

JAMES KIRKUP (1918–)
USA

64

One dog barks at nothing
ten thousand others
pass it on

JAPANESE SAYING

Tomb figure of a guardian dog
China, Late Han dynasty,
1st–2nd century
Glazed pottery

## Full Moon Rhyme

There's a hare in the moon tonight,
crouching alone in the bright
buttercup field of the moon;
and all the dogs in the world
howl at the hare in the moon.

"I chased that hare to the sky,"
the hungry dogs all cry.
"The hare jumped into the moon
and left me here in the cold.
I chased that hare to the moon."

"Come down again, mad hare,
we can see you there,"
the dogs all howl to the moon.
"Come down again to the world,
you mad black hare in the moon,

"or we will grow wings and fly
up to the star-grassed sky
to hunt you out of the moon,"
the hungry dogs of the world
howl at the hare in the moon.

JUDITH WRIGHT (1915–)
Australia

65

## Exchange

Sea gulls inland.
Come for a change of diet,
a breath of
earth-air.

I smell the
green, dank, amber, soft
undersides of an old pier in their cries.

DENISE LEVERTOV (1932–)
USA

Rooster
torch in front
fishing pole behind.

PHILIPPINE SAYING

Bronze bird figure
China, Han dynasty
1st–2nd century

## Sandpiper

The roaring alongside he takes for granted,
and that every so often the world is bound to shake.
He runs, he runs to the south, finical, awkward,
in a state of controlled panic, a student of Blake.

The beach hisses like fat. On his left, a sheet
of interrupting water comes and goes
and glazes over his dark and brittle feet.
He runs, he runs straight through it, watching his toes.

—Watching, rather, the spaces of sand between them,
where (no detail too small) the Atlantic drains
rapidly backwards and downwards. As he runs,
he stares at the dragging grains.

The world is a mist. And then the world is
minute and vast and clear. The tide
is higher or lower. He couldn't tell you which.
His beak is focused; he is preoccupied,

looking for something, something, something.
Poor bird, he is obsessed!
The millions of grains are black, white, tan, and gray,
mixed with quartz grains, rose and amethyst.

ELIZABETH BISHOP (1911–1979)
USA

Bird flies up
where your foot was going

JAPANESE SAYING

## How Birds Should Die

Not like hailstones
ricocheting off concrete
nor vaporized through
jets nor drubbed
against windshields
not in flocks
plunged down into
cold sea by
sudden weather no
please no but
like stricken cherubim
spreading on winds
their tiny engines
suddenly taken out
by small pains
they sigh and
float down on
sunlit updrafts
drifting through treetops
to tumble gently
onto the moss

PAUL ZIMMER (1934–)
USA

Utagawa Hiroshige, Japan
*Sparrows and Wave*, ca. 1828
Woodblock print

67

Lives one day
what does it know
of the seasons

CHINESE SAYING

## Fallen flower I see

Fallen flower I see
Returning to its branch—
Ah! a butterfly.

ARAKIDA MORITAKE (1473–1549)
Japan

Earthworm
little string
through a mountain

PHILIPPINE SAYING

Ma Ch'üan, China
*Beauty on the Shrub*, scroll (details), 1682
Ink and colors on paper

That snail—
one long horn, one short,
    what's on his mind?

        YOSA BUSON (1716–1784)
        Japan

## After the Alphabets

I am trying to decipher the language of insects
they are the tongues of the future
their vocabularies describe buildings as food
they can depict dark water and the veins of trees
they can convey what they do not know
and what is known at a distance
and what nobody knows
they have terms for making music with the legs
they can recount changing in a sleep like death
they can sing with wings
the speakers are their own meaning in a grammar without horizons
they are wholly articulate
they are never important they are everything

      W. S. MERWIN (1927–)
      Hawai'i

## White Turtle

Even though you see me still
    yet I am in motion
Your eyes are deceived
    in thinking I am dead on paper
If you think of ancient creatures
    I am their ancestors
All crawling things have my blood
    I am the only food fit for the chief
    and the chief is food fit for me.
I am the royal heart of wisdom
    that will adapt even to radioactivity
The white turtle am I
    The Most Ancient One is my shell
Tonight I display the symbol
    of your destiny on my back
Tomorrrow I swim back to the deep
    When you are ready pay me a visit
    and recite to me your victories

      KAURAKA KAURAKA (1951–)
      Cook Islands

## Landcrab II

The sea sucks at its own
edges, in and out with the moon.
Tattered brown fronds
(shredded nylon stockings,
feathers, the remnants of hands)
wash against my skin.

As for the crab, she's climbed
a tree and sticks herself
to the bark with her adroit
spikes; she jerks
her stalked eyes at me, seeing

a meat shadow,
food or a predator.
I smell the pulp
of her body, faint odour

of rotting salt,
as she smells mine,
working those martian palps:

seawater in leather.
I'm a category, a noun
in a language not human,
infra-red in moonlight,
a tidal wave in the air.

Old fingernail, old mother,
I'm up to scant harm
tonight; though you don't care,

you're no-one's metaphor,
you have your own paths
and rituals, frayed snails
and soaked nuts, waterlogged sacks
to pick over, soggy chips and crusts.

The beach is all yours, wordless
and ripe once I'm off it,
wading towards the moored boats
and blue lights of the dock.

MARGARET ATWOOD (1939–)
Canada

Which is tail? Which head?
Unsafe to guess
Given a sea-slug.

MUKAI KYORAI (1651–1704)
Japan

## Lizard in Jug

Its small forearms extend to thin points
of fingers. These minute hands printed on white
inside the jug. I thought it was dead.
Then I saw wet bellows puffing out
folds of leather flesh at the armpits.
I looked in the shadows of its eyes,
a fine brush had painted a dark stripe
from eyes to tail on each side.
A lateral flash, it snaked across the water
and hurled itself up to the lip. I reached out
to help it to the ground. It rested its chin
on my finger, we looked at each other,
it was mostly lizard weather.

In the afternoon I felt my spine unlock.
The lizard hadn't used my bridge, it wanted
something more than human. Made a quick S
in the water, smacked its tail on the surface
then airborne leapt to the floor.

I touched its spongy back.
At the beck and call of the small world I wait
practising my sentences for a message from
who can tell where.

SUSAN HAMPTON (1949–)
Australia

## The Tree

I am four monkeys.
One hangs from a limb,
tail-wise,
chattering at the earth;
another is cramming his belly with
    coconut;
the third is up in the top branches,
quizzing the sky;
and the fourth—
he's chasing another monkey.

How many monkeys are you?

ALFRED KREYMBORG
(1883–1966)
USA

Kanō Tan'yū, Japan
*Frolicking Animals*, scroll
(detail), 17th century
Ink and color on paper

# i may be silent, but...

*O*ur finest ideas often come to us when we are alone. Our deepest thoughts we may never express. It is the inner life we are brought back to again and again by poetry and art.

## A Story That Could Be True

If you were exchanged in the cradle and
your real mother died
without ever telling the story
then no one knows your name,
and somewhere in the world
your father is lost and needs you
but you are far away.

He can never find
how true you are, how ready.
When the great wind comes
and the robberies of the rain
you stand on the corner shivering.
The people who go by—
you wonder at their calm.

They miss the whisper that runs
any day in your mind,
"Who are you really, wanderer?"—
and the answer you have to give
no matter how dark and cold
the world around you is:
"Maybe I'm a king."

WILLIAM STAFFORD (1914–1993)
USA

## Silent, but . . .

I may be silent, but
I'm thinking.
I may not talk, but
don't mistake me for a wall.

TSUBOI SHIGEJI (1898–)
Japan

*Guanyin,* China
Northern Sung dynasty, ca. 1025
Wood and polychrome

## The River Is an Island

You are river. This way and that
and all the way to sea two escorts
shove and pull you. Two escorts
in contention.

Left bank or right bank, how can
you be a river without either?

Thus are U bends made. Thus are
S bends made. Your direction
is assured and sometimes running
perfectly and quite straight.

A low bank on your left holds your
laughing stitches in. On your right
side skips another hushing your
loud protests.

*You are river. Joy leaping down*
*a greenstone stair-way: anger cradled*
*in a bed of stones.*

You're a harbour; a lake; an island
only when your banks lock lathered
arms in battle to confine you: slow-
release you.

Robert Dampier, England
*Nahienaena*, 1825
Oil on canvas

Nahienaena, sister of Kamehameha III, was so torn
between traditional Hawaiian values and Western
culture that the conflict broke her health, and she
died in her early twenties.

Go river, go. To ocean seek your
certain end. Rise again to cloud;
to a mountain — to a mountain
drinking from a tiny cup.
Ah, river

you are ocean: you are island.

HONE TUWHARE (1922–)
New Zealand

75

# Night Practice

I
will
remember
with my breath
to make a mountain,
with my sucked-in breath
a valley, with my pushed-out
breath a mountain. I will make
a valley wider than the whisper, I
will make a mountain higher than the cry,
with my will breathe a valley. I will push out
a mountain, suck in a valley, deeper than the shout
YOU MUST DIE, harder, heavier, sharper, a mountain than
the truth YOU MUST DIE. I will remember. My breath will
make a mountain. My will will remember to will. I, suck-
ing, pushing, I will breathe a valley, I will breathe a mountain.

MAY SWENSON (1919–1989)
USA

Porcelain brush rest
China, Ming dynasty
Cheng-te period, 1506–1521

Breast ornament, Fiji, 18th century
Sperm whale ivory, pearl shell, sennit

## Rainstar iii

I saw you once
pinned onto a cloud cushion
and another poet said
that it couldn't be true,
stars don't shine from the center
of clouds,
but he didn't know
you, bright star triumphant.
Rain star generating
morning star promised at
birth
swan star transfigured
moon star mystic
phoenix star rising
from the many ends of the earth.
Wear her light around you
peace within
about you
grace and joy now follow
rise O rise O star

LORNA GOODISON (1947–)
Jamaica

## The Eternal Ego Speaks

Suppose I were a shooting star,
I would want to be seen.
That would be my only meaning.
What is there, after all,
in shooting across the sky
and being burnt up?
But being *seen!*
That would be another thing.

NISSIM EZEKIEL (1924–)
India

Tree grows the way they
    want it to,
that's the one they cut first

KOREAN SAYING


Thread has to go
where the needle went

KOREAN SAYING

## Beware the Man

Beware the man who tries to fit you out
In his idea of a hat
Dictating the colour & shape of it.

He takes your head & carefully measures it
Says "of course black's out"—
He sees himself in the big black hat.

So you may be a member of the act
He makes for you your special coloured hat.
Beware! He's fitting you for more than that.

SAM HUNT (1946–)
Australia

Hat mask, North Luzon, Philippines,
early 20th century
Narra wood blackened and inset
with blue beads

Kanō school artist, Japan
*Scenes of Warriors in Combat,*
17th century
Sixfold screen (detail)
ink and color on gold leaf

Summer grasses
all that remains
of soldiers' dreams.

MATSUO BASHŌ (1644–1694)
Japan

## The Peace Game

"Peace" was a game we liked to play
as kids of six, or maybe seven,
it needs some players to divide
into two teams, of Odds and Evens.
The Odds were the children down the street
and miscellaneous scraps and strays,
the Evens were my brothers and
our friends, swell, upright, regular guys.

"Peace" was the prize the game was fought
(or played, perhaps I mean) to win.
Their object was to keep us out
and ours to get, and then stay, in
for since our fathers didn't want
rough-housing near the orchid sheds,
we fought our battles over their
parents' vegetable beds.

We Evens were a well-fed lot
and tough, so that the little patched
and scrawny Odds would never dare
to say our teams were not well matched.
That was the beauty of the game,
we chose the ground and made the rules,
they couldn't really do a thing
about it, stunted little fools,

Except to put up quite a fight
sometimes against our guns and such.
We called the entertainment "Peace"
or "War"—I can't remember which . . .

YASMINE GOONERATNE (1935–)
Sri Lanka

Keichi Kimura, Hawai'i
*Self-Portrait*, 1939
Oil on canvas

## Forgiveness

Forgiveness is a journey I must take
Alone into my childish fears, and there
Confront my fathers for my children's sake.

I must go back before I cease to care,
And the world darkens and I cannot move.
Forgiveness is a journey from despair

Along a path my ancestors approve.
I must go back and with them make my peace —
Forgiveness is a journey into love.

ALISTAIR CAMPBELL (1922–)
New Zealand

Get there first
and then argue

JAPANESE SAYING

## Chinese Hot Pot

My dream of America
is like *đá bìn lòuh*
with people of all persuasions and tastes
sitting down around a common pot
chopsticks and basket scoops here and there
some cooking squid and others beef
some tofu or watercress
all in one broth
like a stew that really isn't
as each one chooses what he wishes to eat
only that the pot and fire are shared
along with the good company
and the sweet soup
spooned out at the end of the meal.

WING TEK LUM (1946–)
Hawai'i

Dreamed that his pen
blossomed

CHINESE SAYING

Write a bad dream
on a south wall
the sun will turn it into a promise

CHINESE SAYING

## Hope Is the Thing with Feathers

Hope is the thing with feathers
That perches in the soul,
And sings the tune without the words,
And never stops at all.

And sweetest in the gale is heard;
And sore must be the storm
That could abash the little bird
That kept so many warm.

I've heard it in the chillest land,
And on the strangest sea;
Yet, never, in extremity,
It asked a crumb of me.

EMILY DICKINSON (1830–1886)
USA

*Dugong (Sea Cow) and Wildfowl,*
mid-20th century
Arnhem Land, Australia
Bark painting

## So Much Happiness

*—for Michael*

It is difficult to know what to do with so much happiness.
With sadness there is something to rub against,
a wound to tend with lotion and cloth.
When the world falls in around you, you have pieces to pick up,
something to hold in your hands, like ticket stubs or change.

But happiness floats.
It doesn't need you to hold it down.
It doesn't need anything.
Happiness lands on the roof of the next house, singing,
and disappears when it wants to.
You are happy either way.
Even the fact that you once lived in a peaceful tree house
and now live over a quarry of noise and dust
cannot make you unhappy.
Everything has a life of its own,
it too could wake up filled with possibilities
of coffee cake and ripe peaches,
and love even the floor which needs to be swept,
the soiled linens and scratched records . . .

Since there is no place large enough
to contain so much happiness
you shrug, you raise your hands, and it flows out of you
into everything you touch. You are not responsible.
You take no credit, as the night sky takes no credit
for the moon, but continues to hold it, and share it,
and in that way, be known.

NAOMI SHIHAB NYE (1952–)
USA

82

## The Pure Suit of Happiness

The pure suit of happiness,
not yet invented. How I long
to climb into its legs,

fit into its sleeves, and zip
it up, pull the hood
over my head. It's got

a face mask, too, and gloves
and boots attached. It's
made for me. It's blue. It's

not too heavy, not too
light. It's my right.
It has its own weather,

which is youth's breeze,
equilibrated by the ideal
thermostat of maturity.

and, built-in to begin with,
fluoroscopic goggles of
age. I'd see through

everything, yet be happy.
I'd be suited for life. I'd
always look good to myself.

MAY SWENSON (1919–1989)
USA

*Vishnu Standing by a Stream*
Leaf from a *Gita Govinda* series
Aurangabad, India
Watercolor, ca. 1650

## My Happiness

My happiness
    I find
In filling my emptiness.

My emptiness
    I create
In seeking happiness.

GOPAL R. HONNALGERE (1942– )
India

## One Leaping Dolphin Regarding Another, etc. . . . etc. . . .

The music keeps making the shade go up
you can't be secretive
whatever you've got it will show in the universe
whatever the universe has got it will show in you
you don't even have to be intentional
or what used to be called educated
what you've got to do is be born
and that happens as often as it's
necessary for you; some seem luckier,
some seem lovelier, but grace like all
the fish in the sea forever and ever is
something in motion, music, and apparent.

JOHN TAGLIABUE (1923–)
USA

*Boy on a Dolphin*
Syria, 3rd century
Mosaic: colored stone and glass
tesserae mounted in cement

## The Anchor Takes Command

—*for Joseph Feher*

Sometimes there is a weight so full of itself
that it rises, lifting you into an etched sky.
You hold tight out of fear and out of joy
and cannot look down, as it rockets you up
and over an endless expanse of ocean.
Down the years it has gathered to itself
and flies out now, bearded and half-crazed,
wreathed in the seaweeds of its long suffering.
It is propelled by all you would have done without it,
and, because you would have done without it,
it has taken command and will not be left behind.
Now you must cling to it for dear life
for it has lifted you into dangerous clouds
and will not, will not ever, let you down.

   JOSEPH STANTON (1949–)
   Hawai'i

Joseph Feher, Hawai'i
*The Anchor Takes Command,*
1972
Etching

# the minute
# i heard my first
# love story

*f*riendship and love, or the hope of them,

make us glad to be alive, seem to change

the world.

## The Minute I Heard My First Love Story

The minute I heard my first love story
I started looking for you, not knowing
how blind that was.

Lovers don't finally meet somewhere.
They're in each other all along.

RUMI (1207–1273)
Persia
Translated by Colman Barks
and John Maynor

## Straight in the Eye

Straight in the eye
is the way of love,
hate, respect, contempt.
The half-truths look away,
remote as the horizon.

NISSIM EZEKIEL (1924–)
India

*Portrait of a Man and His Wife*
Egypt, Old Kingdom, ca. 2470–2160 B.C.
Limestone with trace of polychrome

## To Be in Love

To be in love
Is to touch things with a lighter hand.

In yourself you stretch, you are well.

You look at things
Through his eyes.
            A Cardinal is red.
            A sky is blue.
Suddenly you know he knows too.
He is not there but
You know you are tasting together
The winter, or light spring weather.

His hand to take your hand is overmuch.
Too much to bear.

You cannot look in his eyes
Because your pulse must not say
What must not be said.

When he
Shuts a door—
Is not there—
Your arms are water.

And you are free
With a ghastly freedom.

You are the beautiful half
Of a golden hurt.

You remember and covet his mouth,
To touch, to whisper on.

Oh when to declare
Is certain Death!

Oh when to apprize
Is to mesmerize,

To see fall down, the Column of Gold,
Into the commonest ash.

GWENDOLYN BROOKS (1917–)
USA

Pablo Picasso, Spain
Two ceramic plates,
ca. 1950s
White stoneware

89

## Heading North

i love you more than a tree full of frogs or
a bursting creek, because you hear loud ants
the scrape of shaving and the sea
making love with rocks.

you leave rainforests where you walk —
parrots and pythons, intricate orchids
slipping from your freckled shoulders
like embroidered gowns.

you don't stop when it stops.
i'm axle to your wheel: careering magpies,
mottled doves, quick flapping away
from the first car for hours

RICHARD TIPPING (1949–)
Australia

Gabor Peterdi, Hungary/USA
*Hawaiian Garden*, ca. 1970
Drypoint printed in green ink

## Sonnet CXVI

Let me not to the marriage of true minds
Admit impediments. Love is not love
Which alters when it alteration finds
Or bends with the remover to remove.
O, no! It is an ever-fixèd mark
That looks on tempests and is never shaken;
It is the star to every wandering bark,
Whose worth's unknown, although its height be taken.
Love's not Time's fool, though rosy lips and cheeks
Within his bending sickle's compass come.
Love alters not with his brief hours and weeks,
But bears it out even to the edge of doom.
  If this be error, and upon me proved,
  I never writ, nor no man ever loved.

WILLIAM SHAKESPEARE (1564–1616)
England

Émile Antoine Bourdelle, France
*Sculptress Resting* (1905–1908)
Bronze

# Losing Track

Long after you have swung back
away from me
I think you are still with me:

you come in close to the shore
on the tide
and nudge me awake the way

a boat adrift nudges the pier:
am I a pier
half-in half-out of the water?

and in the pleasure of that communion
I lose track,
the moon I watch goes down, the

tide swings you away before
I know I'm
alone again long since,

mud sucking at gray and black
timbers of me,
a light growth of green dreams drying.

DENISE LEVERTOV (1932–)
USA

Isami Doi, Hawai'i
*Dreaming Boat*, 1950
Oil on canvas

## Quiet Pain

deep in the shady stillness
of the raintree's thought
i walk blindly into your silence
with you
sitting there like coral rock
your familiar face
is strange

outside
cicada's cry
rekindles the flame
we retreat into ourselves
children of sky and earth
quiet pain lingers like coral dust
we are both afraid to say
i love you as i love you

KONAI THAMAN (1946–)
Tonga

## My Heart

My heart is a lake;
Come and row your boat on it.
I will cuddle your white shadow,
Breaking into jewels against your sides.

My heart is a candlelight;
Please close the window for me.
I will burn myself, quiet, to the last drop
trembling by your silken dress.

My heart is a wanderer;
Play on your flute for me.
I will stay the quiet night through
listening to your tunes under the moon.

My heart is a falling leaf;
Let me stay in your garden a while.
I will leave you as a lonely wanderer
When the wind rises again.

KIM TONG-MYONG (1901–1966)
Korea
Translated by Jaihiun Kim

## Pantun

The precious stone fell into the grass,
fell into the grass and rolled away.
Love is like the dew on the grass:
the sun appears and it is gone.

MALAY FOLK POEM
Translated by Ulli Beier

## Poem

I loved my friend.
He went away from me.
There's nothing more to say.
The poem ends,
Soft as it began—
I loved my friend.

LANGSTON HUGHES (1902–1967)
USA

## Do You Love Me?

Do you love me,
Or do you not?
You told me once,
But I forgot.

ANONYMOUS
AUTOGRAPH VERSE
USA

Ben Norris, Hawai'i
*On the Beach*, 1939
Watercolor

# Silverswords

At cold daybreak
we wind
up the mountainside
to Haleakala Crater.
Our hands knot
under the rough of
your old army blanket.

We pass protea
and carnation farms
in Kula,
drive through
desolate rockfields.

Upon this one place
on Earth,
from the ancient
lava rivers,
silverswords rise,
startled
into starbursts
by the sun.
Like love, sometimes,
they die
at their first
and rare flowering.

JULIET KONO (1943–)
Hawai'i

# Why Don't You Talk to Me?

Why do I post my love letters
in a hollow log?
Why put my lips to a knothole in a tree
and whisper your name?

The spiders spread their nets
and catch the sun,
and by my foot in the dry grass
ants rebuild a broken city.

Butterflies pair in the wind,
and the yellow bee,
his holsters packed with bread,
rides the blue air like a drunken cowboy.

More and more I find myself
talking to the sea.
I am alone with my footsteps.
I watch the tide recede
and I am left with miles of shining sand.

Why don't you talk to me?

ALISTAIR CAMPBELL (1922–)
New Zealand

95

Milton Avery, USA
*Bather on a Raft,* 1944
Oil on canvas

## Labu

When I was a small boy
I played happily on the sand
With my toy canoe, my canoe
    So brightly coloured.

When I became a man like my father,
You pulled my hand away
And I no longer played
With my canoe, my canoe
    So brightly coloured.

You pulled me with happiness
I pulled you with happiness,
We were happy.
On the morrow we fought
And were sad.
My happiness is not like the color of my canoe.

ROBERT SITI (CA. 1948)
Papua New Guinea

96

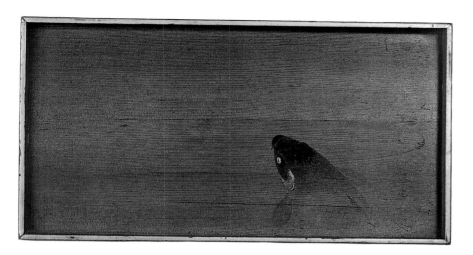

Shibata Zeshin, Japan
Tray for Memorial Tea Ceremony,
1873–1891
Tsuge wood with design in gold and
black lacquer

## To Wang Lun

I was just
shoving off
in my boat

when I heard someone stomping
and singing on the shore!

Peach Blossom Lake
is a thousand feet deep

but it can't compare
with Wang Lun's love
or the way he said
goodbye

LI PO (701–762)
China
Translated by David Young

## Your Catfish Friend

If I were to live my life
in catfish forms
in scaffolds of skin and whiskers
at the bottom of a pond
and you were to come by
    one evening
when the moon was shining
down into my dark home
and stand there at the edge
    of my affection
and think, "It's beautiful
here by this pond. I wish
    somebody loved me,"
*I'd* love you and be your catfish
friend and drive such lonely
thoughts from your mind
and suddenly you would be
    at peace,
and ask yourself, "I wonder
if there are any catfish
in this pond? It seems like
a perfect place for them."

RICHARD BRAUTIGAN
(1935–1984)
USA

97

# what is the opposite of riot?

Some poems surprise us into laughter with their almost-expected rhythm or rhyme or with an unexpected shift of thought that rings suddenly true.

## Some Opposites

What is the opposite of *riot?*
*It's lots of people keeping quiet.*

The opposite of *doughnut?* Wait
A minute while I meditate.
That isn't easy. Ah, I've found it!
*A cookie with a hole around it.*

There's more than one way to be right
About the opposite of *white,*
And those who merely answer *black*
are very, very single-track.
They make one want to scream, "I beg
Your pardon, but within an egg
(A fact known to the simplest folk)
The opposite of white is *yolk!*"

What is the opposite of *two?*
*A lonely me, a lonely you.*

The opposite of *cloud* could be
*A white reflection in the sea*
Or *a huge blueness in the air,*
Caused by a cloud's not being there.

The opposite of *opposite?*
That's much too difficult. I quit.

RICHARD WILBUR (1921–)
USA

Adolph Gottlieb, USA
*Flying Lines,* 1967
Silkscreen

## The Chameleon

People say the Chameleon can take the hue
Of whatever he happens to be on. It's true
— Within reason, of course. If you put him on plaid
Or polka dots, he gets really mad.

JOHN GARDNER (1933–)
USA

## A Fly

A fly
flew in
my last drop of soup.

It grinned when I cursed it
hoping it would drown.

I looked at her
and she simply said —

"Eat your soup
then you can fly."

KAURAKA KAURAKA
(1951–)
Cook Islands

## Haiku

OK, all you frogs
Everyone out of the pond
And form three lines

EDMUND CONTI (1929–)
USA

Jinja Kim, Hawai'i
*Encounter with a Frog,* 1982
Multiple-plate color etching

# Man Alone the Beast

47 million termites
     swarm
     my 60 watt bulb in Kapahulu

I try to love nature
     and nature
     poets tell me wolves
     say, kill
     necessarily, predators
     are non-intentional

     scorpions
     have no Hiroshima
     rats
     no Dresdens
     vultures, Belsens
     barracudas, crucifixions
     nature poets tell me
     man alone
     has killer mind

I try to love
     the food chain
     animal murder
     as transfer of protein

nature
     poets tell me
     calling cops pigs
     insults pigs

whales
     are tuneful
crickets wise
gulls
     screech overviews
monkeys sign direct
     and uncorrupted

nature
     poets say subhuman
     assassination god's
     plan
man alone the beast

so as I spray and spray
my 60 watt bulb
typewriter, desk
and window on Kapahulu
     tonight
I feel
quite natural.

TONY QUAGLIANO (1941–)
Hawai'i

Stop! don't swat the fly
Who wrings his hands,
Who wrings his feet.

KOBAYASHI ISSA (1763–1827)
Japan

Timothy Akis, New Guinea
Untitled, ca. 1980
Ink and color drawing on paper

Timothy Akis gives a description of this untitled work:
"A man is standing over a pig. He has a bird on one
side and a dog on the other. An eel and an insect and
a frog are under the pig."

Marc Chagall, Russia
*The Ebony Horse III*, 1948
From *Tales of the Arabian Nights*
Color lithograph

## Don't Let That Horse

Don't let that horse
              eat that violin

cried Chagall's mother
                    But he
        kept right on
                  painting

And became famous

And kept on painting
                    The Horse With Violin In Mouth

And when he finally finished it
he jumped up upon the horse

                    and rode away
        waving the violin

And then with a low bow gave it
to the first naked nude he ran across


And there were no strings
                    attached

LAWRENCE FERLINGHETTI (1919–)
USA

104

## Riding Lesson

I learned two things
from an early riding teacher.
He held a nervous filly
in one hand and gestured
with the other, saying, "Listen.
Keep one leg on one side,
the other leg on the other side,
and your mind in the middle."

He turned and mounted.
She took two steps, then left
the ground, I thought for good.
But she came down hard, humped
her back, swallowed her neck,
and threw her rider as you'd
throw a rock. He rose, brushed
his pants and caught his breath,
and said, "See, that's the way
to do it. When you see
they're gonna throw you, get off."

HENRY TAYLOR (1942–)
USA

It was when we were winning
that the oar broke

BURMESE SAYING

*A Foreign Groom on Horseback*
China, T'ang dynasty, ca. 8th century
Pre-porcelaneous low-fired pottery

Corn
hides in a cloak
but his beard shows

PHILIPPINE SAYING

Spits straight up
learns something

JAPANESE SAYING

## Painting the Gate

I painted the mailbox. That was fun.
I painted it postal blue.
Then I painted the gate.
I painted a spider that got on the gate.
I painted his mate.
I painted the ivy around the gate.
Some stones I painted blue,
and part of the cat as he rubbed by.
I painted my hair. I painted my shoe.
I painted the slats, both front and back,
all their beveled edges, too.
I painted the numbers on the gate —
I shouldn't have, but it was too late.
I painted the posts, each side and top,
I painted the hinges, the handle, the lock,
several ants and a moth asleep in a crack.
At last I was through.
I'd painted the gate
shut, me out, with both hands dark blue,
as well as my nose, which,
early on, because of a sudden itch,
got painted. But wait!
I had painted the gate.

MAY SWENSON (1919–1989)
USA

Isami Doi, Hawai'i
*Madonna,* 1950
Wood engraving

## Thumb

The odd, friendless boy
raised by four aunts.

PHILIP DACEY (1939–)
USA

## Pillows

I love the ladies with cats on their laps.
The langorous ladies with cats on their laps,
Who seem to be listening twice to what you say,
And fondling, fondling, would never get up and walk away.

Not even if Pavarotti were singing.
Not even if the telephone were ringing.
Not even if you were rude, or cried.
Not even if the cat died.

BONNIE JACOBSON (1933–)
USA

# i thought the earth remembered me

*t*he natural world challenges poets and artists to capture its beauty and variety, the wonder of things being continually reborn. In modern times, as we have become more remote from that world, we realize that nature can be destroyed by mankind. So our poems and art often express an urgent desire to understand, value, and restore our connection with nature.

## Sleeping in the Forest

I thought the earth
remembered me, she
took me back so tenderly, arranging
her dark skirts, her pockets
full of lichens and seeds. I slept
as never before, a stone
on the riverbed, nothing
between me and the white fire of the stars
but my thoughts, and they floated
light as moths among the branches
of the perfect trees. All night
I heard the small kingdoms breathing
around me, the insects, and the birds
who do their work in the darkness. All night
I rose and fell, as if in water, grappling
with a luminous doom. By morning
I had vanished at least a dozen times
into something better.

MARY OLIVER (1935–)
USA

Attributed to Liu Du, China
*Landscape*, scroll (detail),
ca. 1650
Early Qing dynasty
Ink and colors on silk

Ben Norris, Hawai'i
*Mokapu Fisher Village,*
1936
Watercolor

## Behold (E Ike Mai)

Above, above
all birds in air

below, below
all earth's flowers

inland, inland
all forest trees

seaward, seaward
all ocean fish

sing out and say
again the refrain

Behold this lovely world

TRADITIONAL HAWAIIAN CHANT
Translated by Mary Kawena Pukui

## Town and Village

A town is made
of iron, stone, and wood.
A village is made
of palmfrond, people, and great silences.

I am attracted to the villages
but I live in the town.
Why is this? I always
ask myself:

In the town I can hide
from the great silences
that fall at evening.

ALBERT WENDT (1939–)
Samoa

## Looking for Wainiha

One mountain vanishes, and then another,
as rainclouds roll in from the ocean,
and down the range at Hanalei a third peak
loses its place in the new slant of squalls.
How can I tell you where to find Wainiha?

Even the falls darting down the cliffs
will disappear from their vertical tracks
to emerge singing among reeds and moss stone drums.
I can only say that water has its rituals, dark
and inexplicable as the chant of creation.

When you arrive at the twin bridges of Lumahai,
stop for awhile. The double stream will hold you
and tell you a legend of gods seeding the flood,
*male for the narrow waters,*
*female for the broad waters.*

Look past the gingers and plumerias by the swamp—
flowers are for some other time.
Today is the day for acknowledging rain.
See how it floats the mountains and softens stone,
how gently it takes you to the valley of Wainiha.

REUBEN TAM (1916–1991)
Hawai'i

## Hearing the Names of the Valleys

Finally the old man is telling
the forgotten names
and the names of the stones they came from
for a long time I asked him the names
and when he says them at last
I hear no meaning
and cannot remember the sounds

I have lived without knowing
the names for the water
from one rock
and the water from another
and behind them the names that I do not have
the color of the water flows all day and all night
the old man tells me the names for it
and as he says it I forget it

there are names for the water
between here and there
between places now gone
except in the porcelain faces
on the tombstones
and places still here

and I ask him again
the name for the color of water
wanting to be able to say it
as though I had known it all my life
without giving it a thought

W. S. MERWIN (1927–)
Hawai'i

The man pulling radishes
pointed my way
with a radish

KOBAYASHI ISSA (1763–1827)
Japan

Dodie Warren, Hawai'i
*Shanshui*, 1988
Mezzotint printed in blue ink

## *from* High Water

Listen to the rain drop
the underground water
mountain water
tickling
trickling
dripping deep
in the heartbeat
of the massive ranges
black razor edged mountains
with purple peaks
they clutch each other
in perpetual mockery
wild like a tightly packed
formation of warriors
ready to die . . .
high water
of the mountains
seeking the plains
there is no straight path for you
as the crow flies
those rocks defy you
yet you cling from outcrop to precipice
you grind them down
explode them like laughter
like spider's silk you fall
like a poem gliding across
black boulders
convoluting now through plunging ravines
where prawns and crabs gather
carelessly bouncing off the stones

Georgia O'Keeffe, USA
*Waterfall — End of the Road — Iao Valley, Hawaii,* 1939
Oil on canvas

you spray the beauty of creepers
and forms that mimic cliff shapes
the mountain air is trapped
in the solitude of the whirlpool
and the water echoes
the rhythm of rushing feet
like a long column of highland men
seeking the life in the cities below

APISAI ENOS
Papua New Guinea

114

Katsushika Hokusai, Japan
*Great Wave Off the Coast of Kanagawa*, ca. 1820
Woodblock print

## Hokusai's Wave

The two opponents
brace
the wave
gathers itself
slowly climbing the air

and the boat
climbs the vast cliff
of water

steeper and steeper
the endlessly unfolding
fluid and glassy
slopes

but the glittering arch
does not fall
the boat
will not break

there is only one wave
in the universe
and Hokusai is
master of it.

OLGA CABRAL (1909–)
USA

## Surf

Waves want
to be wheels,
They jump for it
and fail
fall flat
like pole vaulters
and sprawl
arms outstretched
foam fingers
reaching.

LILLIAN MORRISON (1917–)
USA

# A GAME CALLED TRYING TO DISCERN THE INDIVIDUAL JOURNEY

A GAME CALLED

TRYING TO DISCERN

THE INDIVIDUAL JOURNEY: or try to keep your eye on

a single wave coming in

pick any wave coming in

go on,

go on,

pick one:

now

try to keep

your eye on

your eye on

your

eye

on

on

it

is            it

still

the very wave

you'd picked?

(for those who do not

live near the sea

use a leaf

or a flake

of snow

fall-

ing

KEITH GUNDERSON (1935–)
USA

116

# It knocks at a door . . .

It knocks at a door of stone
on the coast, on the sand,
with many hands of water.
The rock doesn't respond.

Nobody will open it. To knock is a waste of water,
a waste of time.
Still, it knocks,
it beats,
every day and every year,
every century of the centuries.

Finally something happened.
The stone is different.

Now it has a smooth curve like a breast,
it has a channel through which water flows,
the rock is not the same and is the same.
There, where the reef was most rugged,
the wave climbs smoothly over the door
of earth.

PABLO NERUDA (1904–1973)
Chile
Translated by William O'Daly

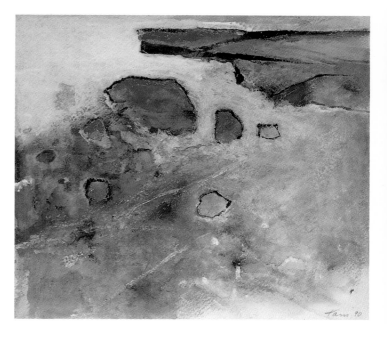

Reuben Tam, Hawai'i
*Islanding: Greening*, 1990
From the *Archipelago* series
Acrylic on paper

The spring sea
rising and falling, rising
and falling all day.

YOSA BUSON (1716–1784)
Japan

## A Stone Souvenir

*"I'd like to get a little stone*
*from your beach to take home*
*as a souvenir."*

Lift it from the tideline, from the hum
of the sea.
The sky will cling to it.

Dark eye of some other time,
round as Io,
unblinking in island wind.

Basalt in its rings, olivine, cinder,
dense, cold,
the cold of the fallen.

And you,
and stone, leaving our island
on the plane tonight,
riding the sky, homeward.

REUBEN TAM (1916–1991)
Hawai'i

Reuben Tam, Hawai'i
*Tidal: Seaweed Pools,* 1989
From the *Archipelago* series
Acrylic on paper

## Pohaku

Water wraps rock
sheening Pohaku,\*
woman of stone flanks,
swirling in eddies
trickling through tidepools.
Here in the splash zone
gobies go darting
past sea cucumbers
lazing and rolling
near the pale seaweed
near the pink urchins.
Hermits are feeding
scuttling old shells,
seaworms' white strings
feeling out each crevice
here in the splash zone
trickling through tidepools
swirling in eddies
blessing Pohaku,
she who chose to be
woman of land
and woman of water,
water
        wraps
                rock . . .

DAWN FRASER (1940–)
Hawai'i

\*Pohaku, according to a legend of Hawai'i, chose to be
part of both land and sea as reef rock, unlike her two
brothers, who left the sea entirely to become land rock.

## Pebble's Story

Wearing away
wears

wearing
away away

A. R. AMMONS (1926–)
USA

119

## I Want an Island

I want an island
where i may be alone
feasting on the sand's
indifferent expanse
here others want to cage me
and i am afraid

there on my island
i will press my feet
into the sand
its cooling particles
will soothe my soul
the seagulls will glide softly
above the pandanus grove
i will feel my printed island
with my eyes
my hands entangled
among the waves
crouching beneath the sky

the one whom I yearn for
is curled against the horizon
at times I cannot help smiling . . .
my island, he's calling me

KONAI HELU THAMAN (1946–)
Tonga

Paul Gauguin, France
*Auti Te Pape,* 1893–1894
from the *Noa Noa* series
Woodblock print

120

Louis Pohl, Hawai'i
*Reef #2*, 1973
From the *Sea* series
Mixed media print

# The World Below the Brine

The world below the brine,
Forests at the bottom of the sea, the branches and leaves,
Sea-lettuce, vast lichens, strange flowers and seeds, the thick
tangle, openings, and pink turf,
Different colors, pale grey and green, purple, white, and gold
the play of light through the water,
Dumb swimmers there among the rocks, coral, gluten, grass,
rushes, and the aliment of the swimmers,
Sluggish existences grazing there suspended, or slowly
crawling close to the bottom,
The sperm-whale at the surface blowing air and spray, or
disporting with his flukes,
The leaden-eyed shark, the walrus, the turtle, the hairy sea-
leopard, and the sting-ray,
Passions there, wars, pursuits, tribes, sight in those ocean-
depths, breathing that thick-breathing air, as so many do,
The change thence to the sight here, and to the subtle air
breathed by beings like us who walk this sphere,
The change onward from ours to that of beings who walk
other spheres.

WALT WHITMAN (1819–1892)
USA

121

## Snail

They have brought me a snail.

Inside it sings
a map-green ocean.
My heart
swells with water,
with small fish
of brown and silver.

They have brought me a snail.

FEDERICO GARCÍA LORCA
(1898–1936)
Spain

Beautiful, seen through holes
Made in a paper screen:
The Milky Way.

KOBAYASHI ISSA (1763–1827)
Japan

## And That Piano

Yes, well I agree
there's been too much
exploitation of resources
but
I like music
and that piano
was once
trees and rocks
and elephants.

ARTHUR BAYSTING (1947–)
New Zealand

Mustard flowers,
no whale in sight,
    the sea darkening.

YOSA BUSON (1716–1784)
Japan

## Proud Songsters

The thrushes sing as the sun is going,
And finches whistle in ones and pairs,
And as it gets dark loud nightingales
        In bushes
Pipe, as they can when April wears
    As if all Time were theirs.
These are brand-new birds of twelve-month's growing,
Which a year ago, or less than twain,
No finches were, nor nightingales,
        Nor thrushes,
But only particles of grain,
    And earth, and air, and rain.

THOMAS HARDY (1840–1928)
England

Joseph Stella, USA
*Sparrows*, 1919
Silverpoint, gouache, and
graphite on paper

123

## Rain on a Spring Night

Congratulations, rain
you know when to fall

coming at night, quiet
walking in the wind

making sure things
get good and wet

the clouds hang dark
over country roads

there's one light from a boat
coming downriver

in the morning
everything's dripping

red flowers
everywhere

TU FU (713–770)
China
Translated by David Young

Elizabeth Keith, England
*A Moro Umbrella, Jolo, Sulu,* 1924
Color woodcut

124

## Rain

I can hear you
making small holes
in the silence
rain

If I were deaf
the pores of my skin
would open to you
and shut

And I should know you
by the lick of you
if I were blind

the something
special smell of you
when the sun cakes
the ground

the steady
drum-roll sound
you make
when the wind drops

But if I
should not hear
smell or feel or see
you

you would still
define me
disperse me
wash over me
rain

HONE TUWHARE (1922–)
New Zealand

Clouds now and then
Giving men relief
From moon-viewing.

MATSUO BASHŌ (1644–1694)
Japan

125

### *from* The Pond in a Bowl

Who says
you can't make a pond
out of a bowl?

The lotus sprig
I planted not long ago
Has already grown full size.

Don't forget,
if it rains
stop in for a visit.

Together we'll
listen to raindrops splash
on all the green leaves.

HAN YÜ (768–824)
China
Translated by Kenneth O. Hanson

Celadon dish with
carved bamboo
Nabeshima ware, Japan,
early 18th century

Leiola Huihui, at age 14, Hawaiʻi
Untitled monoprint

## Coconut

From a far-off island whose name I do not know
A coconut is swept in.

Separated from your native shore
How many months have you been on the waves?

Is the old tree still alive, still flourishing?
Are its branches still shady?

I pillow my head again by the sea,
A lone, floating wanderer.

I take the coconut and hold it to my heart:
the grief of the wanderer is renewed.

Tears welling up in a strange land,
I watch the sun set in the sea.

Endlessly moving tide, feeling with me,
Will I ever return to my home?

SHIMAZAKI TŌSON (1872–1943)
Japan
Translated by Geoffrey Bownas
and Anthony Thwaite

# the afternoon swam by

*O*ne of the main reasons poets write and
artists paint or sculpt is to try to capture
the fleeting beauty in our lives and give it
more lasting form.

Cora Yee, Hawai'i
*Fish Cross*, 1991
Screenprint with
gold leaf

## Afternoon

The afternoon swam by
like a giant fish
with red translucent scales.
In its stillness
the palm trees were copper
and coconuts round
with the clanging of a gong; my eyes
were sweetened
in the orange sifting of oboes.

WANG PHUI NAM (1935–)
Singapore

130

## Beach Rainbow

Heedless of the spray from the steaming waves,
The shell sleeps.
Buried in sand, rolled by the sand shifting as
  the tide shifts,
Not hearing the noise of the thundering waves,
The shell lies down lightly.

Some day, this beach too—
The earth's crust shifting—may turn into fields
Or perhaps into the floor of the sea.

The shell does not worry about the far future,
Does not covet the form of the clouds drifting
  in the sky,
Does not pine after its lost body parted by death.

Idly, not sobbing, not scurrying,
Resigned to the march of nature,
Without anguish, quietly drifting.

In a typhoon, bending its ear to the din:
Baked on the sand in the burning sun:
Picked up by a man in a daydream:
Turned into a button, even.  Unconcerned.

Sea shell,
beach rainbow,
Keep your eyes on your beautiful dream.

> TAKAHASHI SHINKICHI (1901–)
> Japan
> Translated by Geoffrey Bownas and Anthony Thwaite

## A Thing of Beauty

*from* Endymion

A thing of beauty is a joy forever:
Its loveliness increases; it will never
Pass into nothingness; but still will keep
A bower quiet for us, and a sleep
Full of sweet dreams, and health, and quiet
  breathing.

> JOHN KEATS (1795–1821)
> England

Pilgrim flask
(details), Roman
Empire, Syro-
Palestinian coast,
probably Sidon,
2nd–4th century
Blown glass

# To Make the Portrait of a Bird

First paint a cage
with an open door
then paint
something pretty
something simple
something beautiful
something useful
for the bird
then place the canvas against a tree
in a garden
in a wood
or in a forest
hide behind the tree
without saying anything
without moving . . .
Sometimes the bird comes quickly
but it is possible for him to wait years
before he decides
Don't be discouraged
wait
wait if necessary for years
whether the bird comes fast or slow
has no
bearing
on the success of the picture

When the bird arrives
should he arrive
observe the most profound silence
wait until the bird enters the cage
and at that stage
shut the door gently with a putt of the brush
wipe out one by one all the bars
careful not to touch any of the bird's feathers
Then paint the tree
choosing the most beautiful branches
for the bird
paint too the green foliage and the freshness of
   the wind
the dust of the sun
the noise of insects in the grass in the summer heat
and then wait until the bird decides to sing
If the bird doesn't sing
it's a bad sign
a sign that the painting is bad
but if he sings it's a good sign
a sign that you may sign
Then pull out very gently
one of the feathers of the bird
and write your name in a corner of the picture.

JACQUES PRÉVERT (1900–)
France
Translated by Harriet Zinnes

Luana Saffery at age 14, Hawai'i
Untitled monoprint

## Sung

The greenglaze
    Of a Sung bowl held out in the light
Repeats a sea
      On which the haze
Sloping from the hills hangs
    Like still breath.  The shape
Glowing round within the hollow
    Of two hands
    Is an overflow
Of a silence that is bare and whole.
      O it is
A bright achieved silence that sustains
    The morning's
Amaze of light live
    Upon all the wet and dark.
It holds
      An air's
Poise-upon-the-edges-of-things.
    A flawless
Silence it is can catch so roundly
    A gaze
From the thick of crowds
And survive
    Clamors of the wilderness and the loud
  Vanity
    Of open wounds.

EMMANUEL TORRES (1932–)
Philippines

Incense burner,
Lung-chüan ware
China, Southern Sung
dynasty (1127–1279)
porcelaneous stoneware
with blue-green glaze

134

George Peters, USA
*Angels Between Clouds, No. 3*, 1976
Construction

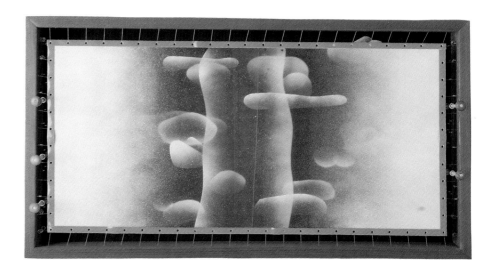

## There Are Poems

There are poems
that are never written,
that simply move across
the mind
like skywriting
on a still day:
slowly the first word
drifts west,
the last letters dissolve
on the tongue,
and what is left
is the pure blue
of insight, without cloud
or comfort.

LINDA PASTAN (1932–)
USA

## The Harp

I lay my harp on the curved table,
Sitting there idly, filled only with emotions.
Why should I trouble to play?
A breeze will come and sweep the strings.

PO CHÜ-I (772–846)
China
Translated by Ching Ti

## Sunset

The sun spun like
a tossed coin.
It whirled on the azure sky,
it clattered into the horizon,
it clicked in the slot,
and neon-lights popped
and blinked "Time expired", as on a parking meter.

MBUYSENI OSWALD MTSHALI (1940–)
South Africa

Lionel Walden, USA
*Luakaha: Evening,* ca. 1916
Oil on canvas

## Evening

The sun horse panting and snorting
Reaches the shores of evening
Kicking his hoofs and flicking red dust
His vermillion mane wet with perspiration
He throws red foam from his mouth

The mellow-colored Evening comes
And places her hand between his pricked ears
Her long fingers
Feel the hot breath from his nostrils
And take off the bridle from his mouth

The restive animal
Tamed and quietened
Walks behind the Evening slowly
And goes into the stable of darkness.

MOHAN SINGH
India
Translated by Balwant Gargi

136

## The Artist

The girl who never speaks
draws a horse like you've never seen,
a horse with feathers,
with eyes cut into diamonds
like the eyes of a bee,
with a tail of braided grasses
and a mane of waterfalls.
Its ears are lilies
and its nostrils homes for swallows,
but its fine hooves and ankles
are what they always were,
because there is no greater beauty.

Where she lives there are no horses,
but she has seen them in books
and watched them rear and whinny
on television. She understands
their patience, day after day,
in the land of the flies. In a dream
she encountered a solitary
blue horse in a field. He came close
and ate an apple out of her hand.

She draws him over and over
in absolute silence. She is afraid
language will fritter away the world,
its gleam and thunder,
its soft, curled lip,
the flying back which only
she dares to ride.

LISEL MUELLER (1924–)
USA

## Horse and Tree

Anyone who's anybody longs to be a tree—
or ride one, hair blown to froth.
That's why horses were invented, and saddles
tooled with singular stars.

This is why we braid their harsh manes
as if they were children, why children
might fear a carousel at first for the way
it insists that life is round. No,

we reply, there is music and then it stops;
the beautiful is always rising and falling.
We call and the children sing back *one more time.*
In the tree the luminous sap ascends.

RITA DOVE (1952–)
USA

Anonymous Kanō School
artist, Japan
*Stable* (uma-ya)
Sixfold screen, ink and color
on paper with gold leaf

# credits

## Poetry

Every effort has been made to locate the holders of rights to the poems in this book and to give appropriate credit below. If there are errors or omissions in these acknowledgments, corrections will be made in subsequent editions, providing the publisher is notified in writing.

"After the Alphabets" and "Hearing the Names of the Valleys" are by W. S. Merwin from *Rain in the Trees*. Copyright © 1988 by W. S. Merwin. Reprinted by permission of Alfred A. Knopf, Inc.

"Afternoon" by Wang Phui Nam is from *The Second Tongue*, ed. Edwin Thumboo (Heinemann Educational Books, Asia, 1976). Reprinted by permission of Wang Phui Nam.

"Always Surprised" and "Water Monster" by Howard Norman are from *Wishing Bone Cycle: Narrative Poems from the Swampy Cree Indians* (Stonehill Publishing Co.). Copyright © 1982 Howard A. Norman. Reprinted by permission of Ross-Erikson Press, 223 Via Sevilla, Santa Barbara, CA 93109.

"The Anchor Takes Command" by Joseph Stanton appeared in *Bamboo Ridge: The Hawai'i Writers' Quarterly*. Copyright © 1987 Joseph Stanton. Reprinted by permission of the author.

"And That Piano" by Arthur Baysting is from *Over the Horizon* (Hurricane House, 1972). Used by permission of the author.

"Another Life" by Dana Naone Hall appeared in *Mana* (Hawai'i Edition edited by Richard Hamasaki and Wayne Westlake), 1981. Reprinted by permission of the author and the South Pacific Creative Arts Society, Raiwaga, Fiji.

"The Artist" by Lisel Mueller is from *Waving from Shore* (Louisiana State University Press). Copyright © 1989 by Lisel Mueller. Used by permission of the publisher.

"'Awapuhi" by Puanani Burgess and "Litany" by Raymond Pillai are from *Mana Review;* "A Fly," "Moana," and "Turtle and Coconut" by Kauraka Kauraka are from *Dreams of a Rainbow;* "Quiet Pain" by Konai Helu Thaman is from *Lagankali*. Reprinted by permission of the authors and the South Pacific Creative Arts Society, PO Box 5083, Raiwaga, Fiji.

"Bats" by Randall Jarrell is from *The Complete Poems*. Copyright © 1969 by Mrs. Randall Jarrell. Reprinted by permission of Farrar, Straus and Giroux and Faber and Faber, Ltd.

"Beautiful, seen through holes . . ." and "Stop, don't swat the fly . . ." by Kobayashi Issa are from *The Penguin Book of Japanese Verse*, translated by Geoffrey Bownas and Anthony Thwaite (Penguin Books, 1964). Copyright © by Geoffrey Bownas and Anthony Thwaite. Reproduced by permission of Penguin Books, Ltd.

"Beware the Man" and "School Policy on Stickmen" by Sam Hunt are reprinted by permission of the author.

"Before We Go," and "Heading North" by Richard Tipping are from *Nearer by Far* (University of Queensland Press, 1986). "Before We Go" was first published by Open Door Press. Used by permission of the author.

"Behold" is from *The Echo of Our Song: Chants & Poems of the Hawaiians* translated and edited by Mary K. Pukui and Alfons L. Korn (University of Hawai'i Press, 1973). Reprinted by permission of the University of Hawai'i Press.

"Birth of Sea and Land Life" is from *The Kumulipo: A Hawaiian Creation Chant* translated and edited by Martha Warren Beckwith (University of Hawai'i Press, 1972). Reprinted by permission of the University of Hawai'i Press.

# Illustrations

## *(in order of appearance)*

Ron Kent, Hawai'i, *Bowl,* Norfolk Island pine, 1988. Honolulu Academy of Arts, gift of Ron Kent, 1988. H. 9¾ in.; diam. mouth 14⅝ in. (24.8 × 37.2 cm).

Koa bowl, Hawai'i, 19th century. Honolulu Academy of Arts, gift of Mrs. Charles M. Cooke, 1931. 9¾ × 15⅛ in. (24.76 × 38.40 cm).

Elizabeth Garrison, USA, *Volcano Dream No. 4,* Pin: sterling silver, copper, glass, enamel, old bone, and cloisonné, 1985. Honolulu Academy of Arts, gift of Helen Drutt, 1986. H. 1½ in.; w. 2½ in.; d. ³⁄₁₆ in. (3.8 × 6.5 × 4 cm).

Anonymous, Courtyard Grille (detail). Honolulu Academy of Arts, 1927. H. 6 ft. 10½ in.; w. 4 ft. 11 in. (209.55 × 149.86 cm).

Madge Tennent, Hawai'i, *Three Head and Shoulders Studies,* blue water-soluble pencil and wash, 1954. Honolulu Academy of Arts, gift of Henry B. Clark, Jr., in memory of Geraldine P. Clark, 1992. 20¼ × 26 in. (51.4 × 66.0 cm).

Ansel Adams, USA, *Roots, Foster Garden,* vintage silver gelatin print, 1948. Honolulu Academy of Arts, gift of Mr. and Mrs. Henry B. Clark, Jr., 1984. 7⁹⁄₁₆ × 6³⁄₁₆ in. (19.21 × 15.72 cm).

Gwendolyn Morris at age 12, Hawai'i, untitled print, 1955. Honolulu Academy of Arts, Linekona collection of student art. 9½ × 12¼ in. (24.13 × 31.12 cm).

Jules Tavernier, France, *Wailuku Falls, Hilo,* pastel, 1886. Honolulu Academy of Arts, gift of Mrs. C. M. Cooke, Sr., 1934. 24 × 35⅞ in. (60.96 × 91.40 cm).

Aztec rattle in the form of a standing woman, clay, 900–1200 A.D. Honolulu Academy of Arts, gift of Mrs. Charles M. Cooke, Sr., 1933. H. 6⅛ in.; w. 3 in.; d. 1 in. (15.56 × 7.62 × 2.54 cm).

Stopper for a lime container, Anonymous Papua New Guinea artist, wood, paint, sennit, and shell, mid-20th century. Honolulu Academy of Arts, gift of Mrs. Philip E. Spalding, 1936. L. 16½ in. (41.91 cm).

Janet Coons at age 16, Hawai'i, untitled collage, 10½ × 13 in. (26.67 × 33.02 cm). Honolulu Academy of Arts, Linekona collection of student art.

Kawanabe Kyosai (Gyosai), Japan, *Vignettes on the Theme Demons and Gods* (detail), ink and color on paper late 1870s. Honolulu Academy of Arts, gift of David W. Hall, 1986. 191 × 9¾ in. (435 × 24.8 cm).

Ann McCoy, USA, *Iguanas*, lithograph and colored pencil, 1979. Honolulu Academy of Arts, 1987. 29 × 41 in. (73.66 × 104.14cm).

Joseph Feher, Hawai'i, *Night of the 'Iwa*, etching, 1978. Honolulu Academy of Arts, gift of Mrs. Fritz Hart, 1992. 17½ × 11¾ in. (44.45 × 29.85 cm).

Louis Pohl, Hawai'i, *Crater #3*, mixed media print, 1972. Honolulu Academy of Arts, 1972. 16 × 22 in. (40.6 × 55.9 cm).

Shōtei Hokuju, Japan, *Monkey Bridge*, woodblock print, early 1820s. Honolulu Academy of Arts, gift of James A, Michener, 1991. 10³⁄₁₆ × 14¹⁵⁄₁₆ in. (25.7 × 37.8 cm).

Doug Young, Hawai'i, *Ahi*, watercolor, 1977. Honolulu Academy of Arts, gift of Artists of Hawaii Fund, 1977. 22¾ × 30¼ in. (57.5 × 77 cm).

Henri Toulouse-Lautrec, France, *May Milton*, color lithograph, 1895. Honolulu Academy of Arts, purchase: C. Montague Cooke, Jr., Fund, 1968. 31⅞ × 23¾ in. (81.0 × 60.3 cm).

Churinga cult stone, Aranda tribe, Central Australia, gray slate with red pigment, pre-European. Honolulu Academy of Arts, gift of Mrs. C. M. Cooke, Sr., 1932. 7½ × 3⅛ in. (19 × 8 cm).

Reuben Tam, Hawai'i, *Islanding: Limestone*, from the *Archipelago* series, acrylic on paper, 1989. Honolulu Academy of Arts, gift of Reuben Tam, 1991. 7 × 8 in. (17.8 × 20.3 cm).

Shibata Zeshin, Japan, *Jurojin, Deer, and Tortoise in Landscape*, color on silk scroll, 1889. Honolulu Academy of Arts, James Edward and Mary Louise O'Brien Collection, 1978. 48 × 17 in. (122 × 43.2 cm).

Japan, life-size suit of samurai armor: iron, leather, lacquer, silk, brocade, and gilding, 1346. Honolulu Academy of Arts, gift of Mrs. Lewis P. Rosen in memory of her husband, 1974.

Joseph Feher, Hawai'i, etching from *Voices on the Wind*, 1955. Used with permission of Alice Feher.

Mary Cassatt, USA, *The Child's Caress*, oil on canvas, 1891. Honolulu Academy of Arts, gift of Friends of Miss Wilhelmina Tenney, 1953. 26 × 21 in. (66.0 × 53.3 cm).

John Young, Hawai'i, *The Red Béret*, oil on canvas, 1945. Honolulu Academy of Arts, gift of the Honolulu Art Society, 1945. 29½ × 23¾ in. (74.9 × 60.3 cm).

Anonymous Inuit artist, Eskimo seal sculpture, steatite, ca. 1970. Honolulu Academy of Arts, gift of Mr. and Mrs. Henry B. Clark, Jr., 1980. 6½ × 1¾ in. (16.5 × 4.5 cm).

Lloyd Sexton, USA, *Three Heads*, pencil drawing, 1952. Honolulu Academy of Arts, gift of C. Montague Cooke, Jr., Print Fund, 1952. 12½ × 14½ in. (31.8 × 36.8 cm).

Shibata Zeshin, Japan, *Monkey Posing as a Collector*, ink and color on silk scroll, ca. 1835. Honolulu Academy of Arts, James Edward and Mary Louise O'Brien Collection, 1977. 13⅝ × 17⅛ in. (35 ×44.2 cm).

Pierre Mignard, France. *Portrait of Three Children*, oil on canvas, 1647. Honolulu Academy of Arts, purchase of the Robert Allerton Fund, 1975. 35 × 46¾ in. (88.9 × 118.7 cm).

Tadatoshi, Japan, *Mermaid*, netsuke, ivory, late 18th century. Honolulu Academy of Arts, gift of David W. Hall, 1985. H. 1½ in. (3.8 cm).

Munakata Shiko, Japan, *Owl on a Branch*, ink and color on paper, 1965. Honolulu Academy of Arts, gift of Dr. and Mrs. Robert M. Browne, 1991. 11½ × 8½ in. (29.2 × 21.6 cm).

Rajasthan, India, *Ganesha*, pink sandstone, 10th century. Honolulu Academy of Arts, 1975. H. 22 in.; w. 16 in.; d. 7 in. (55.88 × 40.64 × 17.78 cm).

Solomon Islands, ceremonial staff (detail), wood, mother-of-pearl inlay, pre-European, Honolulu Academy of Arts, 1935. 51½ × 4 in. (130.8 × 10.2 cm).

Minoru Ōhira; Japan, untitled, graphite and ink wash on paper, 1953. Honolulu Academy of Arts, gift of Jeri Coates, 1987. 37½ × 26⅛ in. (95.2 × 66.4 cm).

Utagawa Hiroshige, Japan, *Asakusa Rice Fields* from *One Hundred Views of Edo*, woodblock print, 1856–1858. Honolulu Academy of Arts, gift of James A. Michener, 1991. 14 × 8¾ in. (33.5 × 22.4 cm).

China, tomb figure of a guardian dog, glazed pottery, Late Han dynasty. Honolulu Academy of Arts, gift of Judge Edgar Bromberger, 1953. 10¾ × 15 in. (27.3 × 38.1 cm).

China, bronze bird figure, Han dynasty, 1st–2nd century. Honolulu Academy of Arts, gift of Robert Allerton, 1956. H. 4⅞ in. (including base); h. 3¾ in. (feet to crest); l. 4½ in. (end of tail to beak) (9.5 × 11.4 × 12.4 cm).

Utagawa Hiroshige, Japan, *Sparrows and Wave*, woodblock print, ca. 1828. Honolulu Academy of Arts, gift of James A. Michener, 1991. 12⅔ × 4¼ in. (32.2 × 10.9 cm).

Ma Ch'üan, China, *Beauty on the Shrub*, scroll (details), ink and colors on paper, 1682. Gift of Mr. and Mrs. Mitchell Hutchinson, 1989. 18¼ × 41¾ in. (105 × 40.7 cm).

Shibata Zeshin, Japan, *Crab Seascape*, light colors on silk scroll, 1881. Honolulu Academy of Arts, James Edward and Mary Louise O'Brien Collection, 1977. 12½ × 16¼ in. (31.5 × 41.5 cm).

Kanō Tan'yū, Japan, *Frolicking Animals*, scroll (detail), ink and color on paper, 17th century. Honolulu Academy of Arts, gift of Robert Allerton, 1952. 24ft 1⅝ in. × 13 in. (735.65 × 33.02 cm).

China, *Guanyin*, Northern Sung dynasty, wood and polychrome, ca. 1025. Honolulu Academy of Arts, 1927. H. 5 ft 7 in. (170.18 cm).

Robert Dampier, England, *Nahienaena*, oil on canvas, 1825. Honolulu Academy of Arts, gift of Mrs. C. Montague Cooke, Jr., Charles M. Cooke III, and Mrs. Heaton Wrenn in memory of Dr. C. Montague Cooke, Jr., 1951. 24 × 20⅛ in. (60.96 × 51.12 cm).

China, porcelain brush rest, Ming dynasty, Cheng-te period, 1506–1521. Honolulu Academy of Arts, gift of Judge Edgar Bromberger, 1952. 4⅞ × 2⅛ × 8¹⁄₁₆ in. (12.32 × 5.38 × 20.47 cm).

Breast ornament, Fiji, sperm whale ivory, pearl shell, sennit, 18th century. Honolulu Academy of Arts, gift of Grossman-Moody, Ltd., 1947. 7 × 7½ in. (18 × 19 cm).

Hat mask, North Luzon, Philippines, narra wood blackened and inset with blue beads, early 20th century. Honolulu Academy of Arts, gift of Mr. and Mrs. Leo Fortess, 1977. H. 4½ in. (11.5 cm); cir. 15½ in. (39.4 cm).

Kanō school artist, Japan, *Scene of Warriors in Combat*, sixfold screen (detail), ink and color on gold leaf, 17th century. Honolulu Academy of Arts, gift of Mrs. Takeo Isoshima, 1989. 24ft 1⅝ in. × 13 in. (735.65 × 30.16 cm).

Keichi Kimura, Hawai'i, *Self-Portrait*, oil on canvas, 1939. Honolulu Academy of Arts, gift of Honolulu Art Society, 1941. 20 × 16 in. (50.80 × 40.64 cm).

*Dugong (Sea Cow) and Wildfowl*, Arnhem Land, Australia, bark painting, mid-20th century. Honolulu Academy of Arts, gift of John Young, 1979. 18¾ × 11⅞ in. (47.7 × 30.2 cm).

*Vishnu Standing by a Stream*, leaf from a *Gita Govinda* series, Aurangabad, India, watercolor, ca. 1650. Honolulu Academy of Arts, gift of Mr. and Mrs. Edward T. Harrison, 1963. 5¾ × 6 in. (14.60 × 15.24 cm).

Syria, *Boy on a Dolphin*, Mosaic: colored stone and glass tesserae mounted in cement, 3rd century. Honolulu Academy of Arts, gift of Hon. Clare Boothe Luce, 1983. 36⅝ × 32¼ in. (98 × 82 cm).

Joseph Feher, Hawai'i, *The Anchor Takes Command*, etching, 1972. Honolulu Academy of Arts, 1973. 12 × 12 in. (30.48 × 30.48 cm).

Egypt, *Portrait of a Man and His Wife*, limestone with trace of polychrome, Old Kingdom, ca. 2470–2160 B.C. Honolulu Academy of Arts, 1938. 20 × 12 in. across back (50.80 × 30.48 cm).

Pablo Picasso, Spain, plates, white stoneware, ca. 1950s. Honolulu Academy of Arts, gift of Mr. and Mrs. Henry B. Clark, Jr., 1985. Diam. 9⅞ (25.08 cm).

Gabor Peterdi, Hungary/USA, *Hawaiian Garden*, drypoint printed in green ink, ca. 1970. Honolulu Academy of Arts, gift of Gabor Peterdi, 1972. 12 × 17½ in. (30.47 × 44.45 cm).

Émile Antoine Bourdelle, France, *Sculptress Resting*, bronze, 1905–1908. Honolulu Academy of Arts, gift of Mr. and Mrs. Richard A. Cooke, Jr., 1988. 26 ¾ × 19⅞ × 13½ in. (68 ×50.5 × 34.3 cm).

Isami Doi, Hawai'i, *Dreaming Boat,* oil on canvas, 1950. Honolulu Academy of Arts, gift of Friends of Isami Doi, 1950. 32 × 40 in. (81.28 × 101.60 cm).

Ben Norris, Hawai'i, *On the Beach,* watercolor, 1939. Honolulu Academy of Arts, gift of Honolulu Art Society, 1939. 15⅝ × 22⅝ in. (39.69 × 57.47 cm).

Milton Avery, USA, *Bather on a Raft,* oil on canvas, 1944. Honolulu Academy of Arts, gift of Roy R. Neuberger, 1950. 26 × 33 in. (66.0 × 83.82 cm)

Shibata Zeshin, Japan, Tray for Memorial Tea Ceremony, tsuge wood with design in gold and black lacquer, 1873–1891. Honolulu Academy of Arts, James Edward and Mary Louise O'Brien Collection, 1977. 7 × 8¼ × 15 ½ in. (17.7 × 20.96 × 39.37 cm).

Adolph Gottlieb, USA, *Flying Lines,* silkscreen, 1967. Honolulu Academy of Arts, purchase: C. Montague Cooke, Jr., Fund, 1969. 30 × 22 in. (76.20 × 55.88 cm).

Jinja Kim, Hawai'i, *Encounter with a Frog,* multiple-plate color etching, 1982. Honolulu Academy of Arts, 1987. 9⅝ × 6 ¼ in. (24.45 × 15.88 cm)

Timothy Akis, New Guinea, untitled, ink and color drawing on paper, ca. 1980. Honolulu Academy of Arts, gift of Dale Buchbinder in memory of his sister, Dr. Georgeda Buchbinder, 1991. 29 ½ × 21½ in. (74.93 × 54.61 cm).

Marc Chagall, Russia, *The Ebony Horse III,* from *Tales of the Arabian Nights,* color lithograph, 1948. Honolulu Academy of Arts, gift of Robert Allerton, 1949. 13 × 17 in. (33.02 × 8.26 cm).

China, *A Foreign Groom on Horseback,* pre-porcelaneous low-fired pottery, T'ang dynasty, ca. 8th century. Honolulu Academy of Arts, bequest of Renee Halbedl, 1981. 6⅞ × 13 in. (17.5 × 33 cm).

Isami Doi, Hawai'i. *Madonna,* wood engraving, 1950. Honolulu Academy of Arts, 1950. 4¾ × 3¼ in. (12.06 × 8.26 cm).

Attributed to Liu Du, China, *Landscape* scroll (detail), ink and colors on silk, early Qing dynasty, ca. 1650. Honolulu Academy of Arts, 1974. 14 in. × 17 ft 3 in. (35.56 × 525.78 cm).

Ben Norris, Hawai'i, *Mokapu Fisher Village,* watercolor, 1936. Honolulu Academy of Arts, gift of Virginia Cowan Hickok in memory of Robert Moffit Cowan, 1986. 14½ × 22 in. (36.83 × 55.88 cm).

Dodie Warren, Hawai'i, *Shanshui,* mezzotint printed in blue ink, 1988. Honolulu Academy of Arts, gift of James W. and Barbara S. Betts, 1991. 6 × 8½ in. (15.2 × 21.6 cm).

Georgia O'Keeffe, USA, *Waterfall—End of the Road— Iao Valley, Hawaii,* oil on canvas, 1939. Honolulu Academy of Arts, purchase: Allerton, Prisanlee, and General Acquisition Funds and a gift from *The Honolulu Advertiser,* 1989. 19 × 16 in. (48.26 × 40.64 cm).

Katsushika Hokusai, Japan, *Great Wave Off the Coast of Kanagawa,* woodblock print, ca. 1820. Honolulu Academy of Arts, gift of James A. Michener, 1955. 10¼ × 15⅛ in. (26.04 × 38.42 cm).

Reuben Tam, Hawai'i, *Islanding: Greening,* from the *Archipelago* series, acrylic on paper, 1990. Honolulu Academy of Arts, gift of Reuben Tam, 1991. 7 × 8 in. (18 × 20.3 cm).

Reuben Tam, Hawai'i, *Tidal: Seaweed Pools,* from the *Archipelago* series, acrylic on paper, 1989. Honolulu Academy of Arts, gift of Reuben Tam, 1991. 7 × 8 in. (18 × 20.3 cm).

Paul Gauguin, France, Auti Te Pape, from the *Noa Noa* series, woodblock print, 1893–1894 (printed in 1921). Impression: Pola Gauguin. Honolulu Academy of Arts Fund, 1938. 14 × 8⅛ in. (35.56 × 20.62).

Louis Pohl, Hawai'i, *Reef #2,* from the *Sea* series, mixed media print, 1973. Honolulu Academy of Arts, 1973. 18½ × 25 in. (46.99 × 63.50 cm).

Joseph Stella, USA, *Sparrows,* silverpoint, gouache, and graphite on paper, 1919. Honolulu Academy of Arts, 1989. 14 × 10 in. (35.5 × 25.5 cm).

Elizabeth Keith, England, *A Moro Umbrella, Jolo, Sulu,* color woodcut, 1924. Honolulu Academy of Arts, gift of Mrs. C. M. Cooke, 1927. 8¾ × 6 in. (22.22 × 15.24 cm).

Celadon dish with carved bamboo, Nabeshima ware, Japan, early 18th century. Honolulu Academy of Arts, 1968. H. 3¼ in.; diam. 12 in. (8.26 × 30.48 cm).

Leiola Huihui at age 14, Hawai'i, untitled monoprint, Honolulu Academy of Arts, Linekona collection of student art. 9½ × 12¼ in. (24.13 × 31.12 cm).

Cora Yee, Hawai'i, *Fish Cross*, screenprint with gold leaf, 1991. Honolulu Academy of Arts, gift of Honolulu Printmakers, 1992. 17¹⁄₁₆ × 20¼ in. (43.3 × 52 cm).

Pilgrim flask, Roman empire, Syro-Palestinian coast, probably Sidon, 2nd–4th century. Blown glass. The Kayyem Collection of Ancient Glass. Gift of Renee Liddle in memory of Faiz Omar El Kayyem and Mrs. Charles M. Cooke, Sr. 1963. H. 7 in.; diam. 4⅜ in. (17.78 × 11.11 cm).

Luana Saffery at age 14, Hawai'i, untitled monoprint, Honolulu Academy of Arts, Linekona collection of student art. 9½ × 12¼ in. (24.13 × 31.11 cm).

Incense burner, China, Lung-ch'üan ware, porcelaneous stoneware with blue-green glaze, Southern Sung dynasty, 1127–1279. Gift of the Honorable Edgar Bromberger, 1950. 4¼ × 5¼ in. (10.8 × 13.3 cm).

George Peters, USA, *Angels Between Clouds, No. 3*, construction, 1976. Honolulu Academy of Arts, 1976. 14 × 24¾ in. (35.56 × 62.86 cm).

Lionel Walden, USA, *Luakaha: Evening*, oil on canvas, ca. 1916. Honolulu Academy of Arts, gift of the Cooke Family, 1935. 44 × 32 in. (114.30 × 81.28 cm).

Anonymous Kanō school artist, Japan, *Stable (Uma-ya)*, sixfold screen, ink and color on paper with gold leaf, Momoyama period, 1573–1615. Honolulu Academy of Arts, 1975. 66¼ × 147¼ in. (168.28 × 374.02 cm); painting proper: 60 × 140¾ in. (152.4 × 357.51 cm).

# index

## Poets and Translators

# Artists

# about the selector

Sue Cowing's poetry and fiction appear in
numerous journals and anthologies. Over
the last thirty years she has studied and
taught Asian, American, and world history
and cultures as well as poetry. From 1989–
1994, she directed an innovative reading
series featuring poets from Hawai'i, the
Pacific, and the continental United States.
The work of some of these poets appears
in *Fire in the Sea*.